FOOTPRINTS ALONG THE WEST HIGHLAND WAY

FOOTPRINTS ALONG THE WEST HIGHLAND WAY

TOMMY RAY

Footprints Along The West Highland Way.

Copyright © 2022 by Tommy Ray.

No part of the book may be used or reproduced in any manner whatsoever without the written permission of the author, except in the case of brief quotations embodied in critical articles and reviews. For information, contact the author at tommy@tommyrayentertainment.com.

Publisher's Note: This is a piece of nonfiction.

Book Cover Design: Judith S. Design
judithsnicolas@gmail.com
http://www.judithsdesign.com

Developmental Editor: Patricia Smith
https://www.linkedin.com/in/patricia-b-smith-035a8813

Editor: Nadia Bruce-Rawlings
nadiarawlings@gmail.com
www.nadiabrucerawlings.com

Map Illustration: Nat Case
INCase, LLC
"Some map data @Open Street Map Contributions"

Book Compositor: Jonathan Sainsbury

ISBNs
Print: 978-1-7326749-4-3
Ebook: 978-1-7326749-5-0

Printed in the United States of America

Also, By Tommy Ray

nonfiction

Rambling Across America
A Quest for St. James

fiction

Mirror of Perception
The Insane Inside
The Feast of the Werewolf
www.tommyrayentertainment.com

Tommy's Music Includes

Crossroads, Angel, Don't Look Back, Push Yourself
Past, Escape, Zama, Passing of the Storm
www.tommyrayentertainment.com

YouTube

Tommy Ray Entertainment – YouTube

GRATITUDE PAGE

This is for those who bring my books to life.

My book designer for this work and all of my publications and short stories, Ms. Judith San Nicolas. She is a woman imbued with creativity and vision. Her contributions to my books have been enormous, and for it, my praises.

TLR

DISCLAIMER

In September 2019, I concluded the West Highland Way, starting in Glasgow, Scotland and finishing in Fort William, Scotland. *Footsteps Along the West Highland Way* chronicled the journey.

Footsteps Along the West Highland Way reflect my opinions related to those experiences. The overall experience was absolutely amazing. From times of aches and discomfort to joy and delight, as well as tears to euphoria because of the overall comradery of the West Highland Way, from friends you meet from all around the world.

I have altered the names along with identifying details of individuals alluded to in the book to preserve their privacy.

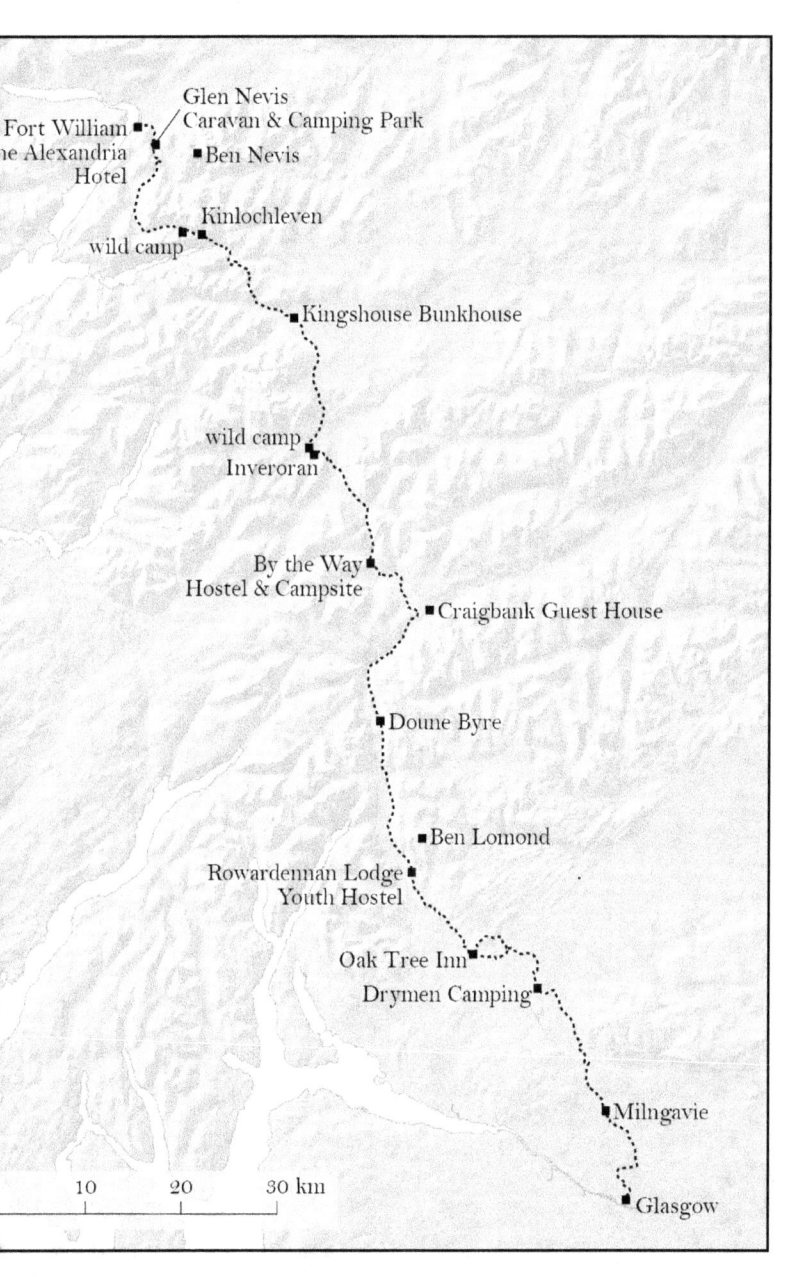

FOREWORD

The travel memoir which follows is the most recent chapter of the "Country Boy" travel memoir series, the third published work by the writer, Tommy Ray. The trip was to Scotland to complete the West Highland Way.

My first trip was the Camino de Santiago, *"A Quest for St. James."*

If you have consistently felt cornered by the drudgery of work and the monotony of life, read *A Quest for St. James.* Let Tommy reawaken your passion for creativity and beauty with this re-creation of his own Camino Pilgrimage.

In that 40-day adventure, shadow Tommy Ray on his transformation from a youthful man with a career to a pilgrim with ideals along the Camino de Santiago. Tommy will sow the seeds of faith and hope in you with his blending of prose and poetic imagery. From scenic vistas, peaceful prayers, to sleepless albergue nights, you will sense the highs and lows of the Camino de Santiago.

I welcome you along the true inspirational pilgrimage, to spark your own inner voice, to leave your mark on the world positively.

The second trip, a self-guided music tour called, "The Confessions of a Dreamer Tour." The publication's title: *"Rambling Across America."*

Rambling Across America describes how I took a dream from an awakened night of slumber and transitioned it into existence. I understood listening to my heart, supporting unwavering faith, and trusting my instincts were more important than what the outside world told me I should be doing.

Imagine living the way of life you have constantly desired. Imagine your dreams coming true. Imagine your fears being conquered. Imagine, after reading *Rambling Across America,* you achieve absolutely everything you desired.

I recreated my life. And so can you.

A prevailing theme for the "Country Boy" travel memoirs was electing to leave behind the amenities of an established way of life to follow my instincts based on a dream to live outside the box. I concluded I was unfulfilled with routines. I was dreaming of adventures grander than existence. I pressed on, living out my creed. I longed to live deeply and abundantly. My excursions established awareness of unbridled liberation. It emanated from my soul.

In addition, it was so exhilarating to discover what was around the next bend, or beyond the river, or to who I might meet in the subsequent hamlet or bistro.[1]

When composing, I had skepticism and uncertainty. What if my memoirs were not drawn out adequately to satisfy a book? What if the narrative was not engaging? Fortunately, when I conveyed my outings, my apprehensions were verified baseless.⁹

"Wilderness appealed to those bored or disgusted with man and his works. It not only offered an escape from society, but also was an ideal stage for the romantic individual to exercise the cult that he frequently made of his own soul. The solitude and total freedom of the wilderness created a perfect setting for either melancholy or exultation."
—Roderick Nash

"Your dreams are never silly, depend on them to guide you."
—Unknown

CHAPTER 1

I was failing in my colossal dreams and had to return to the grind I tried to escape in January 2016. To learn more, read *"Rambling Across America,"* by Tommy Ray.

In late 2016, I transplanted to St. Croix of the United States Virgin Islands and re-joined the routine drudgery of a day job. I continued on the hamster wheel for approximately three years. Sadly, I could not sustain that life. My personal inner conflicts of wishing to live my dream life of Tommy Ray Entertainment vs. the security of a day job was creating anxiety and paranoia attacks.

Imagine you are lying on delicate Turkish sheets. Nightfall darkened the room. You trust the front door and all windows are secured. In spite of that, your grip around your handgun is tight. Your heart is knocking desperately. The tang of horror infused throughout your arteries. These became installments which permeated my existence on multiple evenings.

Though besieged by the Caribbean beauty, I concluded I was unfulfilled with the routine. I was not simply pursuing a vacation, an escape away from something. An expedition was required, a journey towards something. Chasing the restorative and divine convictions of refuge, not to flee, but to discover truth.[1] I felt I had to try anew to live the way of life I sought. I required time to reassess the direction of my existence. My dream of Tommy Ray Entertainment was to be active full-time, my utmost aim. I preferred to be a full-time author, lyricist, recording artist, and create inspiration along with value on my YouTube channel. Besides, I was seeking odysseys larger than life. Life was brief. I wanted to leave positive marks on the world. I yearned to generate encouragement and meaning for the world. The idea of postponing happiness until retirement was wrong. I was too young to settle and be shackled at work. I demanded to unveil yours truly to a new world. A change of scenery was what I was after.

When I realized I no longer could endure on the hamster wheel, I recalled sitting on the sands of my island utopia. I stared upon the heavens, the stars astonishingly clear. It was my moment to embark on a journey to the meaningful pursuit of living. I regarded the treasured bounty from the unfamiliar, an absolute necessity to exert a regeneration of my devastated soul.[1]

To relinquish my position, I had to supply a 6-month letter of resignation because of the inconvenience of replacing me. To maintain an excellent relationship with my supervisor, I presented a 9-month relinquishment.

I recall flying over to his island to aid him with some office cases. Before I had to grab my puddle jumper home, we shared a Chinese lunch. Mid-chew, I sprung it on him. His food at once tumbled from his fork to the below plate. Disheartened by my statement because we had built a superb partnership. He knew my two-year contract was ending. I presumed he was wishing I would extend, not only because of our partnership but the inconvenience of finding someone to settle on my island so far abroad from what most people called normal living.

It was my third time resigning from a position to head out on a quest seeking answers or seeking to kick-start my dream life. For some odd reason, I never asked my employer if I could simply have a sabbatical to go on a long-distant hike to continue my "Country Boy" travel memoir series. To this day, I still do not know why that thought never entered my mind. I concluded I hungered to pursue experiences all over the globe and compose around them.[1] I continued to ponder how I should discover an audience which supports those efforts, so I never had to return to a day job.

My letter of resignation solidified the decision. The next afternoon as I arrived home on the countdown of departure, I researched treks from around the world which would connect me back to nature, supply the insights I wished, as well as be free again. The assumption was correct. My readers, I set the plan in motion without already having a destination.

In a drawer at home, I maintained an assortment of manila folders labeled with the destinations I would prefer to travel to one day. Inside each file were descriptions, maps, guidebook recommendations, special interests about the area, etc. I picked my travels partially because they fascinated and invigorated me. Handling objectives and grasping those challenges empowered me to construct a versatile demeanor, which moreover engaged me to welcome change, confront hardships, and brave uncertainty.[7]

During my research of different treks, there was a 96-mile trek from Milngavie to Fort William, named The West Highland Way. It stretched along multiple lochs, through various mountain peaks and the serene and beckoning Scottish Highlands. It wandered across single tracks as well as open fields of grazing sheep along with cows. The West Highland Way had developed into a pilgrimage for mountain lovers eager to travel exclusively on foot into the heart of the Scottish Highlands. The West Highland Way, an earthly expedition, yet an intimate one as well. The trek was to be a quest in the richest sentiment of the word, a heroic excursion that would revolutionize everything. My soul seared with passion.

As I reflected, a provincial voice in my head retorted, "Sounds neat! Let us do it!" My insides were queasy. The plan was preposterous, but I realized it as the "outlet" I desired to slingshot me from my bewildering course.[1]

I constructed several rationales. Besides improving my health, it was an alluring and thoughtful way to enlighten myself with the scope and charm of Scotland. I would have memories which would endure in my consciousness until the day I perished.1

The trip also provided a valuable experience to find out the ability to protect myself in the wilderness. It would equip me for future treks like the Appalachian Trail or the Pacific Coast Trail or in some new foreign country. I would no longer feel like a nervous toddler. Instead, I would feel like Bryson who penned, "I desired the swagger which came with being able to gaze at a far horizon through eyes of chipped granite and say with a slow, manly, sniff, 'Yeah, I've shit in the woods.'"

And there was a further compelling motivation to go. The West Highland Way was the home to grazing sheep and cows, which one trekked through their territory and could be inches away from wildlife. An experience to truly feel free in nature. They also deemed it a safe, well-marked route.

"Be the change you wish to see in the world"
—Gandhi

CHAPTER 2

I listened to considerable lectures concerning my choices numerous times. It sounded such a bizarre thought to everyone to fly to an unknown land and hike through reality from magazine photographs I had wondered about for half my life. The prevailing question: "why in the name of Sam Hill would you want to do something like that?"[5] Though surprised, it was the third time I had carried out that type of decision.

I had a great job, always 6-figures, yet with my enormous burden of debt, it was more like earning $35,000 a year (praises to school loans). Then after 2–3 years, I resigned to travel on a walk/pilgrimage. Then experienced 3–6 months of being unemployed, which generated even higher debt.

"I rationalized, I reflected; when we are youthful, we have time and energy, but no money. In middle age usually provided energy and money, but no time. And for the fortuitous ones who survive to older ages, many have time and money, but no energy. So, I concluded to move forward when there was a shortage of money."[5]

Being employed in medicine, each day I encountered individuals who perished that day who had no inkling it was their time. It made me aware not everyone reaches an elderly age, let alone reached for their dreams. Besides, if I chose not to go for it, I knew I would regret it on my deathbed someday. To me, it was worth an unknown professional life.

I perceived the undertaking would outweigh the decision to continue a dreary way of life. I would have an unwavering courage. Acquire the adventure of a lifetime. Reestablish a sharp awareness. Witness life in a regenerated illumination. Power the triumph to forge a refreshed energy. Achieve a distinct intention of what I treasured.[9] Remember my readers; one's only job is to enjoy the ride. Every day should be an adventure.

I sought to do things which I never had the thought of doing or had been as reluctant to pursue. Many individuals of the world, as well as companions and family, lived inside a troubled circumstance and would not take the activity to alter their circumstance since they were conditioned to a life of security and congruity, which might show up to provide peace of mind but in reality, nothing was more harming to the bold soul inside a man than a secure future. I believed the delight of life came from our experiences with unused encounters and perpetually changing skyline. I inquired to find all the brilliant things God had set around me to find. An objective of mine was to flow into a completely unused domain of involvement. I had the strength.

Don't disregard major occasions in life which regularly happen as quickly and suddenly as a cloud crosses the sparkling vault of heaven. It will be there one moment and gone the next.[9]

"Knowledge only becomes potential power when applied. Be bold, take risks. I am learning to live between effort and surrender."
—Danielle Omar

CHAPTER 3

I concluded if ever there was a time to experience the Scottish Highlands; it was now. So, I elected to do it. I was doing it for myself. In addition, excitedly, I confessed my purpose to those who knew me. I thus purchased the West Highland Way Guidebook, joined the West Highland Way Facebook Group, and researched through Google Searches. I applied all resources as well from trekkers' accounts who had hiked the Appalachian Trail or Pacific Crest Trail.

At first, I felt immense anxiety and nervousness, which I thought was strange knowing I had trekked the Camino de Santiago in 2012. I had walked almost 600 miles. However, this would be the first trek using a canvas as my sanctuary, cooking over a stove, and, of course, using the restroom in the woods regularly.

Through my exploration of gathering stories, a few

had ghastly tales from hiking the West Highland Way with elevated goals and, shockingly, stylish boots.[7] Trekkers, sorrowfully, retired downcast after a day or two with blisters, or a negative tent experience in the Scottish rains. However, the dominant story was the devilish midges, "annoying blood-suckers." Those tiny flying insects which swarmed and congregated the person in "a diabolical gyrating cloud and intensely bit until the skin was bleeding."[2]

The premiere biting season was from June to August. They yearned to attack at dawn, dusk, long summer twilight hours, and during dull/dreary periods. They were extremely sensitive to light, and they were also susceptible to stagnation on windy or breezy days.

I was told while camping, I should camp on raised ground to increase the opportunity to capture the breeze. When trekking, one's pace could reduce their assaults. If at all possible, wear bright colored long-sleeved shirts, trousers, and a midge-proof head net.[2]

Luckily, I never envisioned myself in those situations to forbid me from advancing forward.

The other negatives were the diseases which a trekker could pick up, such as Lyme disease, as ticks were a major obstacle each day while wild camping.

Remember, ticks painlessly bury their heads under one's skin to feed on one's blood. Lyme disease, if undetected, can remain latent in the human body for years before erupting in a positive fiesta of maladies. The manifestations include, but are not limited to, headaches, fatigue, fever, chills, shortness of breath, dizziness, shooting pains in the extremities, cardiac irregularities, facial paralysis, muscle spasms, severe mental impairment, loss of control of body functions, and—hardly surprising, chronic depression. If one detects a tick, remove it promptly. To remove, use fine point tweezers and grasp the tick where its head pierces one's skin; do not squeeze its body. Tug gently and repeatedly until the tick's legs fall off. After its elimination, keep the area washed with disinfectant.[6]

Trekkers normally walk from South to North. The season usually began in March or April and concluded in early October. The busiest time was June through early September. They considered May the optimal time with pleasant temperatures. The weather was dry, clear, and the flora of wildflowers were out in their full glory. The midges had yet to reach an intolerable level. However, one would have to deal with throngs of people.[2] The negative from June through the end of August was the amount of people along the Way, as well as the relentless midges.

My intention was to leave from Glasgow City on or about Labor Day. I speculated there would be fewer people along the Way and a minimum to no midges. I set aside three weeks for the Way, as well as a few desired side trips.

The precise length of the West Highland Way was 96-miles. Most people used 6–9 days to hike the Way from point to point. The 96-miles was from Milngavie to Fort William.[2]

I was planning to stay in Scotland for three weeks. A couple of days on either side of the West Highland Way to allow sight-seeing in Glasgow. I was also going to start my odyssey in Glasgow, which added 10–12 miles to the overall trip, along with extra side trips. I preferred to ramble along, pausing wherever the day took me.

With the West Highland Way, one had an option with one's luggage or backpack. One could employ a baggage delivery service which transported the gear from stage to stage, or one could pretend to be a tortoise and haul on one's back everything required. I elected to have everything I required within the world resting snugly on my shoulders.5 My intention was to tent camp as much as possible, if not all the way. I envisioned camping would preserve a sense of opportunity and effortlessness which delightfully complemented the act of wandering.[5]

Except for a zone between Balmaha to Rowardennan, a trekker could pitch a tent anywhere, even on private land which many miles of the "Way" covered... As long as one properly camped on private land.

Many employing the luggage services only walked with a light day pack, then retired from the Way each day to a bed-and-breakfast for a hot shower, a hearty meal, along with a soft bed. However, I craved to sleep outdoors and cook my own food as much as possible.

Although I met trekkers with backpacks weighing over 40 pounds, my desired weight was around twenty pounds, which comprised all of my needs, camera equipment, as well as food and water. Sadly, no matter the weight, never for an hour does it escape one's notice, wishing it were lighter.

*"Never say never because limits, like fears,
are just an illusion."*
—Michael Jordan

CHAPTER 4

Through research of ultralight equipment, I recognized how daunting an undertaking it was. The price of each item was high, but I had the basic idea of the supplies and equipment I wanted. I attempted the lightest highest quality item at an affordable price. I could not see myself spending $600 on a tent or $180 on trekking poles, or $300 for a rain jacket. My oldest brother had trekked 200 miles of the Appalachian Trail, so I adopted his basic set-up plus what I researched, requiring if seeking to wild camp along the Way or future long thru hikes. I watched gobs of YouTube videos produced by Darwin, Bigfoot, among others, because they all had walked long thru hikes like the Appalachian Trail and/or Pacific Coast Trail. When I compared their videos to influencers overseas, they were comparable.

When I researched equipment, watched videos, or

read the online articles, it was easy to be simultaneously thrilled and stupefied. I devoted hours researching items. For example, I first typed into Google "best tents of 2019 for ultralight hiking." Then I opened about 10 tabs of websites to compare their top 10 lists as they noted their favorites. After comparing weight, size, and cost, I then searched Google and YouTube for the personal reviews of each one I preferred. Finally, I chose my favorite. I learned about denier high-density abrasion resistant material with single or double walls.

I did that with every item I thought required it. I considered each component due to weight, compactness, and possible multi-functionality. The task took over a month or better during my spare time.

The underlying theme for me personally was weight and price. I read of trekkers filing their toothbrush down to reduce it by a gram. I wanted the highest quality, which would last, least weight, in a cost range. I was comfortable paying for the item. Though as I ordered supplies and piled up my equipment, I appreciated how ounces accumulated into pounds so swiftly.

In 2012, my trek of the Camino de Santiago supplied some insights of weight. During that 600-mile pilgrimage, my backpack remained excruciatingly heavy, especially knowing I slumbered in an albergue (hostel) every night. My pack then, which I carried daily for 35 days, weighed 28 pounds. With the knowledge I had now, the pack could have weighed about 10 pounds.

As the equipment arrived through the mail, I sensed I was shopping for an expedition instead of a short hike of 96-miles. My packing list was a full front and back page.

In the end, I spent around $3,000 on clothes and equipment and could have easily doubled the cost to lessen the weight. My older brother, on the other hand, spent around $1200 for his Appalachian gear.

My goal was to be as light as possible. I knew I only required a few possessions to be safe and comfortable. I tried not to take things, "just in case." I tried to be unyielding with my gear.

I started off with a 60-liter Gossamer Gear pack weighing about two pounds. Normally, the backpack was acquired last once all items were known.

Inside was the following gear:

The most essential item was my footwear. I chose to use lightweight Altra Lone Peak 4.0's. I realized the decision would influence the enjoyment or misery of my walk. Next, I purchased my socks. I chose Darn Tough socks and one pair of waterproof socks. Because of the sloppy conditions, I wore my waterproof socks almost every day. There were days my shoes were saturated, yet my feet were completely dry. To shield myself from pebbles, etc., I wore Dirty Girl Gaiters on my shoes. I also brought a pair of hiking sandals. Sadly, due to them taking a lengthy time to dry, I seldom wore them, even around my campsite. Next trip, I pondered a basic pair of lightweight flip flops.

Based on my readings, September in Scotland could have wet and cold weather conditions. I followed an adaptable layering system to protect myself. The first layer was a thin lightweight t-shirt made from synthetic material. The second layer was a pull-over fleece. My outer layer was a down puffy jacket with an added waterproof rain jacket as needed.

When I arrived in Glasgow, I purchased a pair of long-legged pants to go with the Colombia's shorts. Both were quick drying. I brought rain pants as well. In case of bitter days, I brought Under Armour running tights.

With my plans of camping, I brought a three-season tent, an inflating sleeping pad, and a quilt. I ensured my tent could withstand wet and boisterous weather and netting to keep the evil midges out.

Other items to complete my kit were a titanium pot, a long hand spoon, a water purifier system, a Smart water bottle, a stove and gas bottle which resembled a rocket, a hands-free flashlight which wrapped around my head in case I yearned to mine for gold, and a knife, among other clothes and items.

I had an option of downloading apps and maps to my cell phone; instead, I procured the West Highland Way Guidebook by Charlie Loram. Though it added weight, I simply enjoyed having the book in my hands.

Once everything was obtained, I became enthusiastic and felt a little overwhelmed. I practiced setting up my one-man $275 tent. I unrolled the inflating sleep pad and calculated how many breaths it took, only to read the negative reviews. If using one's human breath to inflate, the pad led to mold. So, I bought the miniature battery pump, which reduced my breaths to 5 or 6 for full inflation. I arranged my sleeping quilt over it and then I lay down for a trial. I imagined myself lying not on my marble floor inside my studio apartment but next to a Loch in the Scottish Highlands, listening to water along the shores, with the wind and tree noise as I blocked out Jason slashing into my tent.

I believed the last time I was in a tent was around the age of 10. I had faith I could manage this.

"Keep close to nature's heart. . . break clear away once in a while and climb a mountain or spend a week in the woods. Wash your spirit clean."
—John Muir

CHAPTER 5

The West Highland Way was the first official long-distance footpath in Scotland. They conceived it in the 1960s. Because of the enormous duties to create such a trek, it did not truly open until 1980. Mostly, the "WHW" was an obvious, well-maintained path with excellent way marks where needed. The way marks were signposts, stone columns, along with wooden posts. The West Highland Way used a white thistle within a hexagon, along with wording. If there was a change of direction, they could have an added yellow arrow. It encompassed the Lowlands and Highlands. It passed from wooded glen to high mountain, along with many habitats in between. The positive of Scotland was the countryside had minimal development with only about eight people per square kilometer in the Highlands. One had an opportunity for a rich variety of wildlife.[2]

Every year beginning in May, about 120,000 visitors came from all over the world to sample the healing balm which came from walking in those less touched places.[2]

The West Highland Way designated a "long distance footpath," was a right of way with open access to the public. Because of the Land Reform (Scotland) Act 2003, established statutory rights of access to land and inland water for outdoor recreation, which came into effect in February 2005. The law now stated there was a right of access to land which was considered, among other designations, moorland, and mountain.[2]

Something new for me while hiking along the Way: there were stiles and kissing gates through boundaries to maintain enclosed grazing areas for livestock.

Most, if not almost ninety-nine percent of the West Highland Walkers, began from Milngavie. Most used the excellent and easy public transportation which Scotland offered. They considered it rather straightforward thanks to a comprehensive network. Scotland offered a national transport system of trains and buses.

A major benefit was many places, one could even leave one's car safely during one's entire walk if one drove to the area.

Another positive of the West Highland Way was no great level experience was required to walk its path, meaning one did not need navigation support because the pathway was well maintained and excellently marked. Plus, one was within a few miles of civilization, or at least a farmhouse, just in case. Most likely, one's cell phone would work along the trail. The only time one might need more experience was if one decided to tackle any side detour trips.

Based on one's schedule, desires, and walking pace, most people used between 6 to 9 days to complete the WHW. As I was planning my three-week trek, I added many side trips and rest days besides the extra days in Glasgow to sight-see.

Most hikers hit the trail in March or April through early October. It was said the best two months are June and September. March and April can still bring unpredictable weather, though through my research I found that in any month one could experience all four seasons in one day. The best things about March and April were fewer hikers and probably no midges, those horrible biting gnats. May was beautiful, but the crowds were invading, and the midges' appetites were growing. If one desired to splurge on hotels and bed-and-breakfast locations, it could be difficult, but if one were a tent camper like myself, then one could go anytime one wished. Definitely consider the midges. July and August brought the hordes of tourists. The weather turned warm and muggy, which of course created the perfect environment for the midges, the worst two months to walk, especially to tent camp.

I went in the beginning of September. I only had one evening during which I wore a head net setting up camp. However, I noticed a lot of the bed-and-breakfast accommodations were filled. The weather was gorgeous, with minimal rain and surprisingly warm blue skies days. If I went again, I would wait until later in September. The issue with the mentioned plan meant most of the places to pitch a tent formally, like a campground, usually closed in October. I would, however, love to see the vivid autumn colors of the highlands. The negative would be more rain and stronger winds. After mid-October still might be doable, the days were shorter, and most places were closed for the season. Besides, if one would like to climb any of the peaks, they might be snow covered, or be more dangerous because of the rain and higher winds.

I was excited. The West Highland Way promised hills, and rocks, and open lands filled with streams, goats, sheep, as well as cows. A bonus was the trail was well marked with limited opportunities to become lost. Plus, wild camping was legal. I was looking forward to the peace and solitude of the Scottish outdoors. Yes, I was pondering "Braveheart."

They documented it. The large and sparsely populated countryside was the closest I could get to true wilderness anywhere in Britain.[2]

"I cannot express how important it is to believe that taking one tiny, and possibly very uncomfortable step at a time can ultimately add up to a great distance."
—Tig Notaro

CHAPTER 6

One blessing of the West Highland Way: NO BEARS. The only bears in Scotland were in captivity at the Edinburgh Zoo, a few giant pandas and sun bears. During World War II, a bear named Wojtek, the Soldier Bear, was the mascot to the Polish troops. He helped carry ammunition at the Battle of Monte Cassino in Southern Italy. After the war, Wojtek spent the last years of his life in Scotland. He died in 1963. Finally, Hercules was an 8 foot, 4-inch grizzly bear bought as a cub from the Highland Wildlife Park. Hercules appeared in films, including James Bond's Octopussy, and TV adverts. He died in February 2001.

The first major importance of the no bears meant I did not have to worry about where I cooked my dinner or stored my food at night. Lying in my tent during a dark evening alone, I did not need to envision the mammoth of a bear moving around my campsite. The sounds of calm snorts, grunts, and growls, and biting would not enter my brain.[7]

It was different for my older brother on the Appalachian Trail. Though John never personally saw one, he had to take precautions nightly. He had to eat away from his camp, ensure his clothes or belongings inside his tent did not have a tantalizing aroma, and he had to hang his food bag in a tree each night to protect it from bear activity. During his 200-mile hike, he heard stories of bear encounters along the Appalachian Trail.

The second major importance was the only thing that could have approached me were sheep, goats, or the occasional cow. Though near the end of my hike, I believe a field mouse which took a nibble from a snicker's bar attacked savagely my hip pocket of my backpack.

Though from my time in the Mississippian or Alabamian woods hunting after dark or walking towards the tree stand before the sun rose, those nightmare thoughts came to life. It was amazing how the mind can play tricks on one in the mysterious realms of darkness. A tree limb or piece of brush can resemble Michael Myers or Freddy in an instance, creating a throbbing heartbeat and a skipping pulse.

Luckily, in hindsight, from my time on the West Highland Way, as I camped, I never had the hot surge of adrenaline, an uninvited shivering within my limbs.[7] Though during my "Confessions of a Dreamer" tour in

2016 (read **Rambling Across America**), I experienced those sensations multiple nights inside my truck when I thought someone was outside lurking around me.

The last important thing I did not concern myself with, though which could have become a reality, were the threats which could happen in isolation. I did not think about falling from a ridge, losing the path within the mist, or losing my balance on slick rocks crossing a stream which could have fractured my skull.8 I read a few stories of people climbing summits unprepared and walking to their deaths.

The West Highland Way had several remote sections, but mostly, one was trekking through multiple towns daily. Besides, I had faith I would always have cell phone service with the combination of interacting with other trekkers daily.

I asked my older brother, who was an avid hiker, to join me. Sadly, he did not have a passport. Instead, similar to my Camino de Santiago trip in 2012, (read, **A Quest for St. James**), I would go alone. However, it did not bother me at all, knowing that on a trip like this I would welcome the comradery of other trekkers daily from all around the world with whom I would interact on the trail and at campgrounds or hostels.

"It is the experiences, the memories, the great triumphant joy of living to the fullest extent in which we find real meaning. God, it's great to be alive."
—Unknown

CHAPTER 7

On the afternoon of September 7th, I departed Tampa, Florida, to set off to Glasgow, Scotland. My oldest brother, John, drove me to the airport. It thrilled him for me, as he knew his next Appalachian Trail adventure would ensue in April 2020.

Upon arrival, I could see in his eyes he wished he were traveling with me. After shaking hands adieu, I strolled into the terminal. My gut turned; a great vitality overcame my body.[5] In my hands were my backpack along with an extra daypack, which kept my camera equipment, journal, guidebook, prescription glasses, and travel documents.

The double glass doors automatically opened upon my approach. I placed the backpack on the scale of my Lufthansa flight terminal check-in, displaying nine kilograms. I was happy I satisfied the airlines' weight limit and kept the weight of my pack below 14-pounds; unfortunately, they considered a 60-liter backpack an oversized piece of luggage, so the $60 fee applied making the backpack checked-in luggage.

Check-in moved smoothly as she placed the proper luggage tag and provided me with my boarding pass. She stated, "have a wonderful trip." I was off to the gate, first via the escalator, then onto the train which transported me from the main airport to my terminal and gate.

The initial flight to Frankfurt, Germany, had an 8-hour flight time. I plopped down into my aisle seat. In the blink of an eye, the flying machine maneuvered along the Tampa runway. The plane lifted off the ground. Thunder from the turbines propelled us into the heavens. Turbulence bumped my harmony as the plane shivered.[5] Once above 10,000 feet and beyond, the flight flattened out into a smooth ride. I passed the time watching movies, along with multiple naps. A thought sparked, "I was astounded, once again, by how simple the act of taking off was and how great it felt. My world returned suddenly to being wealthy with opportunity."[5]

The inflight services treated me well with delicious meals and snacks. I could have sampled plenty of red wine or champagne, however, I behaved and remained with water.

Upon arrival in Frankfurt, a three-hour stopover awaited. We had to deboard to rain laden skies. We had to maneuver a few football fields on foot before loading our bus to the terminal. Luckily, I had my rain jacket to diminish the saturation. Sadly, Frankfurt, Germany, did not offer a Priority Lounge to relax in. Instead, I spent the time wandering through the various shops, gazing upon the local delicacies and souvenirs. I swapped a few American dollars to acquire lunch as I waited for the final two-hour flight into Glasgow. The minutes ticked as I observed people from around the world discovering new or old places. My innards bubbled with a fervor. I knew my trip was to be a journey in the abounding sense of the word. An epic jaunt to alter everything.[5]

Upon landing in Glasgow, the alloy tube grounded and navigated to a stop on the airstrip. I departed the plane and headed into the terminal.

When I arrived in Glasgow, I did not know what to expect. Coming from a Caribbean island where I had not felt temperatures below 72 degrees Fahrenheit in over three years as well the past few weeks in the heat and humidity of Florida, I imagined a shock to the system. I recalled when friends of mine living in Florida would visit me in North Carolina during the fall months with 50-degree temperatures; they were wearing bulky ski jackets because of the temperature changes. I imagined it would be the same here in Scotland for me. However, when I exited the airport, the air temperature of 55 degrees Fahrenheit was delightful. Through my tinted prescription glasses and blue eyes, I scanned the outside sky. I ventured out of my life into an energizing world. I trusted I would have encounters which would distinctively live in my mind until the day I passed on.[5]

One positive aspect about Scotland was English was spoken. It was a simple task to ask for proper directions to assure I found my bus and access to the hotel in the city of Glasgow. I had had a much more arduous time on an earlier adventure when I landed in Paris, France, because of the language barrier on my Camino de Santiago pilgrimage, (read, *A Quest for St. James*).

Outside of the airport was a straightforward path to their public bus system to accommodate travel from the airport to one's required destination. I purchased my ticket and awaited my turn to board. As I ascended the three metal steps to the older gentleman sitting behind the wheel, I mentioned the rarity of public transportation for me. I informed him about my hotel and asked to assure I did not miss my stop. With a friendly grin, he winked and, using no words, I felt relaxed. I sat a few rows behind him in a window seat to scan the landscapes as we ventured into the unknown.

The double decker public bus whisked from the airport into the city of Glasgow. There were a few people with backpacks surrounding me. I wondered if they were there for the West Highland Way as well, or perhaps simply traveling around. I had regularly heard it was simple to travel around the European countries because of their transit systems. Though I trusted my driver, I kept a keen eye on the stops to ensure I exited at the proper site. I have consistently been rather nervous on public transportation to ensure I did not become lost or confused.

During the excursion, I recalled passing over a small body of water which resembled a river. The darker hue of water was calm, and it appeared to vanish in the distance. On the horizon were mountain ranges. I was curious if I would scale those at some stage.

After what may have been about a thirty-minute comfortable ride, the bus halted and dropped me off at George Square, about a half a mile from the Moxy Glasgow Merchant City Hotel, my home for the next couple of nights. I had to be dropped off shy of my destination because of street construction.

George Square, the principal civic square in Glasgow, named after King George III and laid out in 1781. Today, the Glasgow Square was home to the headquarters of the Glasgow City Council, and exhibited an extensive collection of sculptures and monuments, including those dedicated to distinguished Scots such as Robert Burns, James Watt, Sir Robert Peel and Sir Walter Scott. The Square served as the venue for many popular events. Perhaps the best thing about George Square was its location. It was located perfectly amid the city's notable boutiques, bars, and restaurants, so it was easy to discover something to do after having taken in Glasgow's historical highlights.

I stepped from the bus onto the concrete sidewalk. As I observed my surroundings, I put the daypack over my shoulders and placed my backpack in my left hand.

I was exuberant with energy. I typed into Google Maps the name of the hotel and started my trek. The initial eye-catching sight was the enchanting appearance of the Glasgow City Council Building. Its stone carved architecture reminded me of a building I encountered along my Camino de Santiago trip in Spain in 2012. The square itself appeared to be a delightful and tranquil place to unwind. It was a popular ground for an afternoon lunch or coffee break. Surrounding the plaza were the mentioned above statues and many beautiful buildings around the square. It was surprisingly clean, despite all the crowds visiting.

I began walking east along the sidewalk. I limited my strides due to carrying the backpack in my left hand, along with trying to gaze upon the sights. On my right side were shops, bakeries, and local grocery stores. The left side was bustling with cars speeding through in both directions to unknown destinations. At each block's intersection, I paused and wait for the correct walk permission sign to ensure I did not become flattened by a non-looking driver or, worse, a double-decker bus. I recognized a mixed aroma of diesel fuel, garbage, fish and chips, along with the passing perfume of a lovely young lady.

When I reached the Moxy Glasgow Merchant City Hotel, I checked in with a warm welcome. A positive I loved about the hotel. One had to use the key in order to go to one's room. There was a scanner on the wall of the elevator. I liked the security which was offered. Stepping off the elevator, I entered my room. I opened the window as it faced west. Gazing over the direction I had just walked, I arched my back with a long deep breath stretch, thinking I had been up for almost 30 hours except for a few cat naps here and there on the flight. I dropped my bags and quickly unpacked everything I could. I then slipped into a lavishly steamy shower, inserted myself between crisp white sheets (how long would it be till I enjoyed that kind of comfort again?) then channel surfed, noting no NFL football. My exhausted eyes closed as a deep slumber fell upon me.

"Life moves pretty fast. If you don't stop and look around once in a while, you could miss it."
—Ferris Bueller

CHAPTER 8

Glasgow, "Second City of the Empire," known as a fascinating and lively place. Similar to most cities, Glasgow contained top museums and art galleries. Added to the arts was the Glasgow Cathedral, restaurants for all tastes, as well as a vibrant nightlife. The city of Glasgow dated back to 1125. By the 18th-century, it had become a major Centre for international commerce. They highly recommended it in the guidebook to spend a couple or few days in Glasgow, either before or after the West Highland Way.[2]

"Remember, then: there is an only time that is important, and it is now! The present moment is the only time when we have any power."
—Tolstoy

CHAPTER 9

After two days of rest in Glasgow, sight-seeing, it was time to finish purchasing foodstuff and supplies, as I would take off the next morning. I first wandered to an outdoor store, Tiso Glasgow Outdoor Experience. I needed a pair of hiking pants, cooking fuel, and protection against the savage midges. The store was located at 50 Couper Street. Upon entering, it reminded me of an REI store back in the USA. It had anything and everything one required, undoubtedly. Plus, the store associates were all thoroughly helpful, especially in the midge's protection area.

Last, I continued to the supermarket to obtain my provisions for the first few days on the Way. I had researched meals and types of food for cooking. Unfortunately, I used an Alba. Many of the desired choices were not available. As I pushed the shopping cart around aisle to aisle in pursuit of nutritious lightweight food, I would snag a few staples I had read about. I purchased two packs of pepperoni with mozzarella cheese, couscous, porridge bars, Snickers, crackers, along with cashews and pistachios.

I understood eating nutritiously on the trail was possible. Though grabbing goodies which packed a lot of calories is advisable as well. If you research most of the nutritional intake of a hiker on the AT trail, you will feel like a teenager again eating all the worst foods available but savoring every bite.

After the check-out, it overwhelmed me with the weight of the items I had bought. Three days of food appeared to weight around 4–5 pounds. In reality, it probably only topped out at 2 pounds. Strolling back to the hotel it delighted me I had intelligently selected proper choices of what was available. Sadly, though, I concluded I still ended up with too much.

Once in my room, I began the packing process. I laid out all things I was trekking with. I wished to put blue eyes on it all to ensure each item was in its proper place, ditty bag, or pouch. The 60-liter backpack became my life-support system.

"Be your own artist and always be confident in what you are doing. If you are not going to be confident, you might as well not be doing it."
—Aretha Franklin

CHAPTER 10

GLASGOW TO MILNGAVIE

Walking from Glasgow to Milngavie was definitely suggested. It initiated at the Centre of Glasgow at the Kelvingrove Park. It was an added ten miles (16 km). The initial impression was plodding along polluted asphalt aside to bustling streets. Instead, the Kelvin and Allander rivers, parks and beside fields were the reality.

A quote I appreciated was by Thich Nhat Hanh, "Walk as if you are kissing the Earth with your feet."

The TV was blurry when I woke up to a darkened chamber. I leaned over to my right side to view the crimson digits on the hotel's clock: 5:45 am. I scrunched my toes into the carpet and arched my back. Staggering across the room, I opened the drapes to view outside and noticed the pavement was wet with a moderate downfall of rain. The streetlights illuminated the skies. My stomach growled with roars of breakfast desires. A benefit of the hotel was they offered a complimentary morning meal. A superb first step to power my energy before leaving. The guidebook stated there was nowhere on today's route to obtain food or drink until about two miles from my destination, a pub called The Tickled Trout.

After devouring two plates of scrambled eggs with beans and orange juice, I returned to the room with a stuffed belly. I finished the last steps of preparation to leave for the last time. I enjoyed a lengthy hot shower, then a final review to ensure I had everything packed and was positive I did not need to use the restroom before departure.

I stepped outside with an endearingly innocent pulse of excitement, wearing my rain jacket and pants. I promised myself with an uncommon insight not to get insane with covering mileage–my wish was to embrace the encounter, not to be obsessed with the arrival.

I heaved my rucksack and took a rearward wobble, amazed by the heaviness of the burden of an approximately 30-pound backpack. My intention originally was to have a 15–20-pound backpack which comprised my camera equipment, food, along with water. I had failed miserably. I yanked tight the hip belt and shuffled off. The rain downcast me a little. Nevertheless, I knew to expect rainfall practically daily. September averaged over eight inches of rain for the month. Besides, tales of experiencing four seasons in one day were common knowledge.

With the rain descending, prepared to ramble. For that day, I had been waiting for months. I knew individuals would creep themselves to work, stranded in rush hour, enveloped in hazed pollution, or sedentary behind a work area longing to be some place else. I was going on a journey through the Scottish Highlands. I was more than prepared for it. Ahead of me spread a tremendous, new world.[5]

I had a two-mile trek through the downtown streets of Glasgow to the Kelvingrove Park, where the trail initiated. Over 95% of the West Highland Way hikers began 12 miles ahead of me in Milngavie.

As I walked first through the city streets, I noticed how my hotel was on the opposite side of town from the starting point. Another added negative. Layered with clothes because of the temperature and rain; sadly, I began to sweat shortly into my walk. I halted once to remove a few layers. I did not realize my body would heat so rapidly when walking with my pack.

As I strolled those two miles, I witnessed hundreds of people trudging to work. The rain was picking up in intensity.

I thought about how Glasgow grew upon my interest as a future home. Not merely because it provided anything and everything you could want, but it likewise provided the walkability I had invariably desired.

When I arrived at the Kelvingrove park, I was uncertain where the path started. There was a maze of concrete routes in multiple directions for the daily active locals to walk and ride their bikes. I looked side to side, searching for the east bank where the trail should be. To lessen my anxiety, I paused at the centerpiece of the park; a fountain chiseled from stone. The fountain had various bronze statues around its base, with a woman on the centerpiece about twenty-five feet above me. I asked a local woman who was escorting her small white dog in the near vicinity to point me in the correct direction of the path. With a quick point of her left index finger, I was on my way.

I advanced nervously onto the path. An intense feeling swelled in my chest, and a lump formed in my stomach. I took a huge breath. And with that, I started strolling.[7]

The way led down onto a cemented pathway with a bubbling stream or river, the River Kelvin. The path was primarily flat and woven below the city. The skies were overcast with a slight sprinkle. Because of the mild temperatures and moisture, everything at ground level was green and flourishing. Once I was on the route, I noted well-marked signs to assure the correct direction. The day was September 9th, 2019. I was on my way.

Glasgow was high above the river, and the concrete passage produced a tranquil environment. The river itself was murky brown, rapidly flowing along. The earliest structure I noticed for history was the Kirklee Bridge. January 1900 is when the foundation stone was established. I seemed to be the sole trekker with a backpack, yet several joggers, bikers and dog walkers either passed me or crossed in the opposite direction in those first moments.

Because of the added rain gear under the pack I carried, I could feel sweat beading up along my spine. The material of the rainwear intensified the heat, as if I were in a private sauna. I was wearing an under t-shirt and a long sleeve type shirt. Remember, I had stopped a mile after leaving the hotel and removed my outer fleece and puffy jacket. I wished I were shirtless. Though warm and icky along my back, I trudged on. I was reluctant to eliminate too many items and become cold when I paused for breaks.

As the day advanced, I continued to think, how did my backpack come so heavy? The steps were not a struggle, yet my shoulders throbbed within the first four miles. Sadly, I had another eight miles to go. I approached a bench along the path, so I halted for a brief refreshing water break. I was blessed. I could access my Smart Water bottle without removing my backpack. For the brief pause, I left my pack on, only to enjoy a few sips before proceeding on. With the pack I used during the Camino de Santiago trek, I had to remove the full pack each time I required water.

After my brief break and a couple of miles of walking, I arrived at an area called Maryhill. Unfortunately, I became confused. It seemed I was to leave the path along a side road and continue to a road which transitioned into the countryside section. I turned left, but I surmised I should have continued right. I walked through an office parking lot, then ended up tramping around a complex which had numerous soccer fields. Though on an established path, I did not think it was the West Highland Way. I came upon two gentlemen after passing over a walking bridge where a professional soccer club was practicing. They pointed me straight ahead to the main road, the A879.

Or perhaps I chose the correct way and made my error at the A879.

When I arrived at the A879, I followed it, a busy highway, into town, though there was an underlying blessing. My stomach gurgled.

According to the guidebook, I should have navigated over the A879 then crossed the Balmuildy Bridge, which was a footbridge which would have brought me on a path along the Allander Water.

Sadly, my body wished I could stop around the seven-mile mark. The last time I humped a backpack of that weight was in 2012 for the Camino de Santiago (read, **A Quest for St. James**). Indeed, although I don't have children, one could envision walking along with one's young child on one's shoulders for around 5.5 hours nonstop. It aches greatly. Contemplate strolling with the weight for hours, for days, and not along level black-top paths with seats and snack booths at helpful interims but over an unpleasant path, full of sharpened rocks, as well as astonishing inclines.[5]

I continued strolling with a slight lean with a stout backpack, marginally slouched, and pushed forward because of weariness and achiness. I used my trekking poles as much as possible to relieve the strain of the weight.

I had read stories of people crying after one day, but that was the first day after Milngavie. As mentioned previously, minimal trekkers travel from Glasgow to Milngavie by foot. Nonetheless, the entire trek was voluntary. Unlike a long thru-hike analogous to the Pacific Coast Trail, most people finished the West Highland Way.

In hindsight, I was supposed to cross that busy four-lane road to engage the riverside trail. Unfortunately, I remained next to the A879. I walked along the bustling highway for about an hour as I adhered to the signs to Milngavie. The positive — I had an emergency demand for a bathroom. Luckily, a restaurant, the Tickled Trout Pub, was open and allowed me to use it. I peeled off my sweaty clothes and relieved my stomach discomfort. After dressing again in the moist cloth, I continued along after thanking the establishment.

Around 3:00 pm, I turned right, which was onto the Main Street of Milngavie. I shuddered my backpack onto a bench and rested there, sipping water, and devouring a Snickers bar. Next to the bench were children playing on a swing set. People were enjoying the outside dining as others were simply walking around tackling their errands. I was the only hiker amongst everybody.

The rain ceased, but the skies remained grayish. I stripped down to my dampened T-shirt. The long-sleeved shirt could be wrung out at the sleeved ends. I rested for about ten minutes, then went up to search around. There was a maroon phone booth and the monument to display the start of the West Highland Way. They likewise had a sign banner over a bench where I had observed many snapped their pictures from. A bridge over a running stream helped the ambience.

Unluckily, a tad of anxiety mounted. First, the store in my guidebook, The Iron Chef, which I wished to visit, was no longer open. It was on the For-Sale Market. Second, the campground I was planning to stay my first night in was over a half mile away, and I could not reach them by phone or by website to ensure it was available. I pondered if I should walk to it anyway or consider alternative options. Please take a moment to realize my cell phone was from the USA. My plan granted me to text and use the internet as often as I needed. Sadly, phone calls would cost $0.25 a minute, plus maintenance charges.

I scanned my guidebook. There was a popular bed-and-breakfast, the Best Foot Forward, about two-tenths of a mile away. So, I strapped the hefty backpack back on and followed the Google Map directions. As I reached the home, I found it was desolate. I rang the doorbell and knocked on the door. As the time was nearing 5:00 pm, I felt uneasy. I called the number, straight to voice mail. I remained another twenty minutes before moving to option two, a local hotel. There were three in the area, according to Yelp. One, completely booked, the other advised me the cost would be over $120 an evening; even though the website reported $80. For an unknown reason, I could not book the cheaper price online. Finally, I contacted the other hotel, the Premier Inn, by phone. They granted me an $80 rate. They were located about one mile outside of town, from the same direction I had previously been. I left the unmanned bed-and-breakfast and listened to Google guide me to my bed for the night. The negative was I was retracing ground I thought I had gratefully put behind me forever.

I found the Premier Inn, settled behind a Scottish Pub restaurant and a McDonalds. Even though I was craving a Big Mac, when I travel abroad, I do my best not to succumb to eating from local fast-food favorites I easily can have in the USA.

I entered the hotel, and someone completed the registration. I was thankful. My shoulders were achy. Though I had originally planned my first night to be in a tent, I was welcoming a hot shower and queen-size bed to spread out on.

Upon entering the room, I unpacked all of my belongings. I was pondering ways to reduce my weight, if at all feasible. Afterward, I took a lengthy hot shower to remove the tough day's trek.

For dinner, I chose the Scottish Pub Restaurant. There, I reveled in a pint of a local IPA along with a steak supper. Overall, the dish was pleasant to my taste buds. Finishing the last morsel, I paid off my bill and retired to the hotel. I was considering laundry, but they did not provide public washers or dryers. I had been wearing the same clothes now for four days.

Back in the room before turning in, I repacked my backpack and lay out clothes for the morning. I crawled into bed underneath the white sheets and closed my eyes. With the warmth of the room, a final sigh, I gave myself to slumber, inquisitive about what more was out there.

CHAPTER 11

MILNGAVIE TO EASTER DRUMQUHASSLE (DRYMEN)

It thrilled me to begin the new day. It filled me with excitement and anticipation of a new revelation. The sole task which was not exciting was the application of the backpack. Once again, I had allowed myself to over-pack, making for myself a future of discomfort.

The day's stage, considered the initial stage for most hikers of the West Highland Way, was about a 12-mile jaunt.

I retraced my steps that morning to the launching point of the West Highland Way. I stepped to the obelisk, a stone marker about 8-feet in stature which formed a pointed tip. Engraved in black block lettering was "West Highland Way." Being it was September 10th, 2019.

Only eight other hikers led off by the time I was there. We helped each other snap photos at the starting stone monument and banner before departing Milngavie. In my photo, my yellow Lone Peak trail runners stood out against the grayish contrast of the obelisk. If I have done the walk in June or August, I was told there could be hundreds of hikers along the same starting pathway.

Milngavie was a middle-class commuter suburb on the northern edge of Glasgow. At the initial start of the route, there was a small pedestrian Centre which possessed plenty of shops and restaurants. Like yesterday, it overflowed that morning with people shopping, running errands, and children playing over at the playground.

One requirement was finding an ATM. The guidebook mentioned stocking up on cash here.

After my photographs, I took a deep breath, told myself, "I can do this." I adjusted my backpack and began.

I paused shortly after leaving the obelisk at a rusted metal structure with two trekkers painted on it stating, "West Highland Way, One of Scotland's Great Trails." As I began, I noticed immediately the locals enjoyed the initial part of the Way as an exercise haven. It was a straightforward landscape of delicate paths through convenience parks and forests. People were escorting their dogs, walking in general or mountain biking through the saturated dirt trail and small water puddles.

The automobile traffic was detectable in the distance from the city. There were charming sounds, the gurgling of running water by the trail, forming small rapids created by the Allander Water/River.

As I rambled along, I considered a deviation at the Mugdock Country Park. It bore the remnants of the Mugdock Castle dating back to the 14th century and the Craigend Castle built as a residence in 1815, which were likewise in ruins. Sadly, I missed the detour, a fingerpost sign in the Mugdock Wood. So, I proceeded on the main path, escaping the suburbs out into the genuine countryside.

My first needed rest break was at the Craigallian Loch. My yellow trail runners were no longer bright from the smears of mud. Yet this was expected from the many tales I read planning for Scotland. Luckily, the day was cloudless, with blue skies and pleasant in the sixties. The Loch was lovely. I found a dry space to sit and nibble on a protein bar and an apple as I noticed a few anglers in their row boats aiming for local trout. The water had a Guinness stout hue, a considerable contrast from the pristine Caribbean Sea my eyes had gazed upon for the preceding three years, where one could see the bottom even at 100 feet.

Departing the Loch, I passed the Craigallian Fire Memorial. The site became notorious in the 1920s. It was an informal meeting place for a range of passers-by that included travelers, climbers, walkers and the unemployed fleeing the Great Depression in Glasgow. People stopped, assembled around the fire, consumed tea, and told stories.[2]

Upon the trail, I had to cross over a stone wall. The marvelous aspect was the stunning views of the Campsie Fells, the Volcanic Conical Hills of the wooded Dumgoyach and Dumgoyne beyond. The weather sadly did not oblige me to gaze upon Ben Lomond, which marked the start of the highlands. Another aspect I learned quickly in Scotland was how the weather changed. They informed me one could encounter all four seasons of weather in one day, depending on one's location. Within the start to my current location, after a couple of hours, the temperature only marginally lessened, but the skies went from a heavenly blue toward a ghostly haze of drab.

As I continued on through a valley then into farmland, I originally sought a pit stop at the Glengoyne Distillery. I wished to sample a local whiskey even though I was not a fan. I tried a sample Bourbon tray at a bar in Philadelphia in 2013 and sadly could not get past the third sip. However, I learned the distillery had a 12-year-old Highland single malt, which was greatly recommended. Unfortunately, when I reached the detour trail, because of being tired already, I chose not to trek over to it even though it was visible in the distance, about a mile away. My words of wisdom to all travelers, do not listen to the voice which says, "you are tired, do not go." The regret sucks. Take those extra steps for the experience. The guidebook even claimed it would be a discredit to pass without a quick stop and a revitalizing wee dram.2 Well, the guidebook was correct, damn it!

My next break occurred at the Beech Tree Inn, stationed a mile or two further up from the Distillery. The pleasant feature about the Beech Tree was the trail ran past the back door. The Inn was not a place to reside, rather to eat, have a drink, or to observe the wildlife they had in enclosures and surrounded horses. Unfortunately, I arrived after the kitchen had closed. Instead, I sipped a Coke and snacked on my own food for my rest break, relaxing on one there many wooden picnic tables.

Up to that moment, I had not crossed paths with anybody who was on the same course. The original individuals I met at the starting point all went off before me, and since I walked only about two miles per hour, I typically caught no one. While at the Beech Tree Inn, I noticed a few people sitting around, but it was hard to say if they were hikers, since there were several automobiles in the parking lot, and I did not notice any backpacks except mine.

I sat alone at my outdoor table, somewhat shivering. The heat generated from walking dissipates quickly. A lesson I recommend is to have a puffy jacket handy when pausing or setting up your campsite.

I wrapped up my momentary rest, shouldered my rucksack, and advanced towards my cheerful landing place.

The next objective was to locate the Drymen Campsite. It was before entering the township of Drymen by roughly two miles, considered Easter Drumquhassle. A major selling point was the cost, only 5 pounds a night, which included a hot shower.

Between the Beech Tree and the impending campground, the skies opened to a drizzle, common Scottish weather. Another quick lesson was the number of little streams I had already passed over. There was no need to carry vast amounts of water. I could readily have access to water anytime I desired it. I would only need to filter it to be safe. Yet I had read people consumed it straight from the streams with no ill effects.

As I proceeded to walk along fields of lush pasture lands, I sensed the campsite was an elusive target. With a combination of the miles, the weight of my backpack, and the ongoing uphill battle of the asphalt roadway, my body was nearing its breaking point. The trail was turning out to be more challenging for me than I had originally thought. Even a home offering refreshments and ice cream with an honesty box did not lift my spirits.

About another mile down the road, I approached a home on my right which offered camping by their barn for three pounds. The signs showcased fire rings as an added bonus. Yet, stubbornness continued my strides.

I treaded up the final asphalt hill in the misty skies. Ultimately, I discovered the sign for the Drymen Campsite. It was an elongated small field, similar to an "L" shape, with already about twenty tents set up. I first coursed through the protected space with the bathrooms, showers, and a makeshift kitchen. There were more people there than I expected. The cost was 8-pounds instead of 5 from the guidebook. Inside the sheltered area, people assembled around in plastic chairs or at the few available picnic tables. The hiss of camp stoves on the countertop with threads of soaring food smoke, the three outlets filled to capacity with chargers and phones. Most of the people were in their twenties and seemed to be from varied countries because of the languages I overheard. I passed through to spot a place for the evening. On the top edge of the clearing by a small fence, thinking the slope would help with the rain falling down. My tent did not have a deep bathtub, and I preferred not to be flooded or wet in any manner. There were three tents on my sides and I had six feet from them. I erected my Six Moons Design Skyscape Trekker tent quickly upon the ground as it was more dirt and mud than grass as the precipitation and wind strengthened. I could not put down the ground sheet because of the wind. Instead, I arranged it over the floor of my tent, thinking it could still act as a barrier to help with dryness. I tried to bring my belongings inside and me without too much mud or rain inside my tent as I crawled in. I learned quickly a one-man tent does not have considerable room for a person and a backpack. Plus, my tent used my trekking poles to support it. I kept hitting them with my knees and my pack, causing me to lose the apex of my tent from time to time. I was clearly a newbie at tent camping.

Unfortunately, the slope was more than I hoped. With the combination of the material floor of the tent and the substance of the Therma-rest inflatable Neo Air, it was like lying down on an ice rink. I quickly slipped to the end of my tent. My feet brushed against the tent material, leaving about 8 or more inches of distance up by the head region.

Another task to overcome was the unpacking of the backpack. I had observed countless videos on how to pack it in the first place, and the universal lesson to store your sleeping gear was at the bottom. So, what did that mean? I had to take out every item inside my backpack to get to it. After 12 miles, unpacking 20 pounds of gear in a semi-kneeling position listening to the rain strike the polyester material of the tent, suddenly, I was quite fatigued. After forming the tent into a little home, I lay supine to understand what it would be like for the evening. My feet pressed against the single panel sloping tent. I modified and tried to construct a well-balanced platform. I arranged my backpack to my left to prevent me from slipping against the side of the tent and placed the remaining items at the foot to prevent me from pressing the tent. I was fearful by touching the tent I would invite condensation onto my quilt. I did not wish to awaken to wet feet, or a ruined brand-new quilt.

Once I collected myself, I found my sandals, towel, and wash zip lock baggie and headed for a hot shower and to use the bathroom. The shower was surprisingly powerful and hot. After a full day's trek, I loved the grooming experience immensely. It impressed me as well as my fellow trekkers. I was apparently the tenth or more person to pass through the shower, and it was rather clean. There was no grime or leftover body hairs to be seen.

The negative of the first paid campsite was there were no laundry services as previously advertised. Unfortunately, they had not opened up those services yet. I had been wearing the same clothes for about four to five days. I should have completed a load at the hotel back in Glasgow before departure.

After the shower and dry night clothes, I snatched my food supplies and headed into the commons area to eat. A positive about the Drymen Campground was the eating space. It allowed one to relax at picnic tables and be neighborly with people from other countries. Another positive, one could remain dry no matter the weather as one ate. One only had to bear the elements from the safe haven to the tent, which could be as little as 10 yards to the length of a football field depending on the tent placement.

My first time operating a camping stove with fuel was amusing. I accidentally caught my steel wool on fire. When I started the fuel for cooking, I had it too close to the flame. I did not know it was so easily flammable. I had read steel wool was an outstanding way to clean your cooking pot after you ate.

Tonight was also my first experience eating a dehydrated backpack meal. The chicken and pasta dish sounded tantalizing on the package. After pouring the water inside and allowing it to dehydrate, I sat at a picnic table with Alexander, a gentleman from Belgium. He was in his late 20s and hiking alone as well. His English was limited, and my Dutch was nil; so we predominantly sat in silence, preparing ourselves for the forthcoming meals. Sadly, I must have added too much water or other error, like not waiting enough time. It was gooey and not appetizing. After two bites with a grumbling belly, I tossed it in the trash. Instead, I heated a packet of soup coupled with a Snickers bar. I wrapped up the evening with a cup of hot tea. Ultimately, nowhere near adequate calories for the day's expenditures of energy. During my hike/walk of the Camino de Santiago in 2012 ("**A Quest for St. James**"), I dropped approximately 15–20 pounds over those 600 miles. I was trying not to repeat the same weight loss program. I merely stand 5 feet 6 inches. At the start of the trip, I was at 145 pounds.

Upon completion of my meal or instead my snack, I hurried back to my tent to lessen my exposure to the elements of rain. I crawled into my tent, keeping my water bottle and head lamp nearby. I shimmied into my liner and quilt, profoundly grateful I was horizontal, warm, and presently dry.

Shockingly, I could not sleep. With every movement, sounds erupted from my Neo-Air. In addition, I could hear my neighbors coughing, talking in various languages, snoring, and body movements, all of which kept me preoccupied.

As the night progressed, a smashing storm ensued. Thirty to forty miles per hour winds and gusts with a monsoon pouring down. As I attempted to remain settled in my den of a tent, the rain fly was fluttering in the battering storm. Each wind-driven drop sounded like a dynamite blast.5 I lingered diligently on my raised sleeping pad and watched my tent and remained curious about its durability. Finally, because of exhaustion, my eyes closed, and I escaped into a dreamless trance.

"Everything you ever wanted is one step outside your comfort zone."
—Unknown

CHAPTER 12

EASTER DRUMQUHASSLE TO BALMAHA

When I awoke, at first, the interior of my tent appeared to be dry. Even though I tossed and turned most of the night, I remained on top of my inflatable air pad. There was a small amount of condensation on the single panels of the tent. I knew from my reading to try not to touch those panels because it would allow the water through the porous material. I remained snug in my quilt and was in no rush at all to begin the day, so I simply remained supine. I listened to my foreign neighbors move about through zippers, clicking of buckles on backpacks, along with stretching grunts.

After a while, the outside sounds diminished. I became aware I should act and perform the tasks of packing. I planned to walk at least seven miles.

I unfastened myself from my nylon womb and surfaced. Presently, the skies were rainless, however dreary, displaying a possibility of added showers. The temperatures were mellow and reviving. It satisfied me to be absent from the hot, sticky Caribbean. I put my Lone-Peaks on, and I mingled with the remaining trekkers, arching my back like a cat.[5]

I collected my belongings, taking inventory. Irritated, I noticed about a half of a cup of water inside the tent. With the slope, it had all pooled in one small part of my tent, which protected my belongings from becoming saturated. I was curious if it was due to not putting down the ground sheet first and the water had penetrated from underneath. Was it the higher winds which wafted water inside through the single panel, or was the tent leaking from a seam? I was dry, my quilt was dry, but I was concerned proceeding forward with further tent camping planned.

Another additional aspect I noticed was the hatred of stowing away a wet tent. Afterward, my hands and arms were wet and muddy, and I was afraid of producing a moldy, smelly home. They advised me to stop some place during the trek if the sunlight exposed itself and allow it to dry. Typically, those ultra-light tents dried quickly in the appropriate setting.

Before taking off, I dined on a porridge bar, a few nuts, a Snickers bar, and water. Once camp was all gathered, I hoisted my full pack and set off once again.

Departing, I was alone with my backpack. Virtually everybody from Drymen had already exited the campground. The remaining few were housed in their tent longer or were sitting at the picnic table enjoying their hot breakfast.

That day, I prepared to walk to Balmaha. It was a seven-mile, (11km) distance. I was on the verge of the Highlands.

I moved in silence, slowly at first along the country lane with a misting rain starting. I paused a few moments over the initial mile to snap photographs of the lush landscapes with the mountains of Loch Lomond and Conic Hill on the horizon, which I would scale in my future. Along the road were edible blackberries on which I foraged.

The city of Drymen, though off the route, was the first town I could have encountered, about 1.5 miles from the campground. It was a larger village. Many trekkers used the city as their first night along the Way. I bypassed it and continued my route. Eventually, I reached my first access gate. Those gates were throughout the Highland Way. They served as a portal, separating pasturelands, and prohibiting animals from crossing into areas they should not be or into other adjoining properties. The rule was to assure one closed it behind one.

After crossing through the Garadhban Forest, a previous conifer plantation, I paused temporarily for a peanut M&M snack. I rested upon a concrete bench by a small stream with a backdrop of birch trees. An endless hush dominated the countryside.

I had to choose. I had a decision of two routes. The easier track descended into Milton of Buchanan, which followed the pavement by the B837 highway for approximately two miles to Balmaha. The other higher route was to ascend Conic Hill after passing over moorland. They considered it strenuous, yet rewarding. Other tempting reasons to choose the higher trail were the Highland Boundary Fault. It was a massive geographic fracture dividing the Lowlands from the Highlands. And, when standing on top of Conic Hill, the views allowed one to see the line of islands across Loch Lomond clearly marking the direction of the fault zone, which stretches right across the width of Scotland from Kintrye to Stonehaven, just south of Aberdeen.[2]

I chose the higher track to maintain natural paths through open moorlands towards Conic Hill. As I advanced on my trek, the weather deteriorated, with declining temperatures and heavier rain. The winds howled. The path was muddy, forming an ice rink surface. Due to free sheep grazing land, one had to watch one's step for their feces. Luckily, I was wearing my waterproof socks inside my LonePeaks. Though my shoes were saturated, my feet were warm and dry.

I ended up crossing a few streams along the trail. Once again, if one chose the West Highland Way, water, to that point, was easily found. No need to weigh oneself down with too much water weight.

Eventually, I began my first substantial climb. The incline increased by 550 feet. It supplied wonderful moorland views, yet did not prepare me for the impending Conic Hill climb. The manual stated a five-minute walk to the top. Unfortunately, the ascent was to 1184 feet in a brief distance.

As I began the climb upwards, the path was like a rock staircase. As the elevation advanced, the wind started strengthening its velocity. I rambled skyward like an overworked aged yak. At some point I wavered, my throbbing thigh muscles recaptured some vitality, but after only a spattering of more strides, my pace weakened once again. In any case, I urged my hurting self and called forward all of my stores of energy.[5] The pauses were not all bad, as I inhaled fresh pure Scottish air overlooking pastureland crowded with sheep and saw multiple trekkers chasing me to the summit.

Behind me, I noted a light tapping on the way. It sounded effortless and musical as a Kentucky Derby winner running around the backstretch to victory. Then swiftly, out of nowhere, with a swish, a streak of sodden track shoes and long legs zoomed by me as simply as a Porsche passing a feed wagon. He kept going and going until he peaked the ridge and vanished. I immediately felt old for a split moment. I went on climbing until I reached the summit.[5]

The wind was whirling along boisterously and relentlessly at a vigorous thirty miles an hour but gusting to at least double that. Originally, I aspired to camp up there.

There was no way to pull it off. I could relish in the panorama views for about ten minutes. Loch Lomond, Ben Lomond, and the Arrochar Alps were sensational. I gazed below upon the massive green meadows populated with the sheep below. I grinned as I was leading a rich and thrilling existence in that present moment. I wished to remain longer. Sadly, the winds made it unreasonable to linger.

The descent was tricky. I had to be careful not to stumble in the mud and steep rock steps with the sustaining gusting winds. Being Conic Hill, many people surrounded me, well over a hundred. Most were arriving from Balmaha and using it as a short-day trip. A bunch of students dressed in jeans, sneakers with limited jackets were enjoying a field trip escaping their classroom.

I continued my descent into Balmaha. With shoulders aching and becoming hungry, I paused at a grassy knoll which overlooked a distant Loch to recapture my strength.

I arrived in Balmaha. Balmaha was a smaller village created around a loch shore, where many residents anchored their boats. It likewise served as a departure site for cruises to explore the chain of islands stretching across Loch Lomond. By the water was a sculpture of Tom Weir, a local legend.

I paused at the automobile park associated with the National Park to figure out my next move for housing. The car park was the launching grounds for the day trippers.

Allegedly, there was a campground nearby, but I could not locate it. I attempted to check into a bed-and-breakfast, but all were full. Instead, I dwelt in the Oak Tree Inn. The room was 65-pounds for a nightly stay. Near was a Village Shop for snacks and a few items for walkers to restock. The Inn provided a restaurant with breakfast included.

I retired to my room after checking in. I stood beneath the steady stream of the shower, the hot water wiping away the day's travels. Afterward, I hung my tent up to allow it to dry out along with all of my belongings.

I strolled over to the restaurant and relished in Scottish meat pie while savoring a local draft beer. After my tummy was full, I exited. I visited the store for a few things like snickers and breakfast bars, along with a soda. Up to that time, I had not seen a Dr. Pepper during my Scottish visit.

Back in the room, I cranked the heat to 75 degrees and tugged the blankets up to my chin. I was cozy and protected. My eyes slid closed.

On those travels, it did not bother me to have minimal contact with others. I enjoyed my alone time.

"The only way we can change the way we feel is by realizing our inner experience and learning to befriend what is going inside ourselves."
—Bessel A. VanderKolk

CHAPTER 13

BALMAHA TO ROWARDENNAN

I roused from slumber and entered the Hotel for a hot breakfast, which was covered in my stay. It was buffet style to serve yourself. The choices comprised scrambled eggs, beans, (a Scottish tradition and norm for breakfast), a type of pork which appeared undercooked compared to how we serve it in America, as well as my first experience of Haggis.

Haggis, according to the Britannica interpretation, was the national dish of Scotland. A type of pudding comprising the liver, heart, and lungs of a sheep (or other animal), minced, and mixed with beef or mutton suet and oatmeal and seasoned with onion, cayenne pepper, and other spices. The concoction then packed into a sheep's stomach and boiled. I was told they could serve it in a heavy whiskey sauce or serve it like a sausage patty.

As I raised the silver top, I detected a liquid dark sauce with unknown contents. It appeared soupy. Because of seeing the murky liquid, I instantly closed the top. I detected no odor, nor did I wish to explore the silver container to see what Haggis may look like.

Overall, it was splendid to start the day with a hearty hot breakfast instead of a cold porridge bar. Afterward, I returned to my quaint room to pack for the day.

As I took off from the hotel with my belongings upon my back, I paused for a moment at the Tom Weir statue. They regarded him as Scotland's Most Loved Mountain Man.

He was a Scottish mountaineer, author, as well as a broadcaster. He was best recognized for his lengthy-running television series Weir's Way. Mr. Weir was a pioneer for preserving the Scottish environment. He loved meeting people as well as exploring the landscapes of Scotland. On December 29th, 1914, he was born and died on July 6th, 2006, in West Dunbartonshire, Scotland.

Today, I prepared to walk to Rowardennan. It was 11 km, (about seven miles), over lovely terrain. I would stroll along the "bonnie banks" of the Loch Lomond for most of the day.[2]

Departing the statue, I began the morning along a concrete path parallel to Loch Lomond. The path allowed me to observe the boatyard and jetty. Across the Loch was an island nature preserve, Inchcailloch. It was a wooded island which could be visited by boat at any time of the year. There were nature trails for hiking, pointing out the natural and human history of the island. Most people liked to visit in spring when the bluebells and primroses were in blossom. They translated Inchcailloch into "Island of Nuns." It was given the name because of its association with Christianity and St. Kentigema. St. Kentigema was a missionary from Ireland who settled on the island in the 8th century. They established a church on the island in the 12th century. Upon one trail, one could see the remnants. Another bonus was the island granted camping.

Loch Lomond was the grandest area of fresh water in Britain. It was 37-km, (23 miles), long; up to 8-km, (5 miles), wide; as well as 190-m, (623 feet), deep near the Rowchoish Bothy. It was created by a glacier over 10,000 years ago. There were over thirty-eight islands in it. The Loch was famed for giant pike.

Eventually, after a mile or so, the concrete path transitioned onto the beach. The fresh perspective provided stunning views and ambient sounds. I relished the serenity; however, it was sadly brief. The path returned to the main two-lane winding road. Luckily, in September, it was not hectic. However, I read in the summertime; it was rather chaotic with holiday tourists.

I entered a narrow patch of Birch, Rowan, Oak, and Scots Pine after walking for a while. The melodies of birds whistled to me, welcoming me as the morning progressed. The skies were overcast, but not too chilly.

Only moments later, I arrived at Cashel Farm. Cashel was the "Forest For a Thousand Years." It was the ambition of Cashel Farm to revive the 3000 acres of native woodland. The ultimate objective for the restoration was correcting the destruction which we humans had done to the environment.

As I approached the Cashel Caravan and Campsite around 10:30 am, I paused and performed laundry. Laundry was a perk instead of a burden. It has been roughly seven days since I had washed my clothes, which meant I had worn a few of my items for seven days straight. I was alone in the laundry room, so I stripped down completely and put on my rain gear so I could wash my entire inventory of clothes. Laundry took about an hour and a half to complete. As I rested in my chair watching the clothes go round and round, I pondered, "I was seeking harmony. I proclaimed I was required to attain it amidst myself and this province.5" The blessing was now the application of warm socks and underwear as I departed back into the milder temperatures. I could also fill up my water bottle and snag a snack in their store.

Outside the Cashel Campground, I had to succumb to a stiff 90-meter (295 feet) climb. The trail was boggy from earlier rainy days. The rest of the trail meandered through beautiful native woodland punctuated by rocky coves, along with tiny beaches. I managed to peer underneath into a ghostly void. Past a canopy of petals was a splendid glimpse over the flawless Loch Lomond. The scenery was untamed.

I arrived at my destination of Rowardennan. Rowardennan itself was a tiny settlement. It offered a hotel, the Hostel, a restaurant or two, and a Lodge. I stayed at the Rowardennan Lodge Youth Hostel. It resembled a Victorian hunting lodge.

The Hostel itself offered no vacancies. Instead, I camped around the corner along the Loch. The charge per night was an 8-euro fee. The benefit of the charge was I could also have the value of the Hostel amenities. Inside, they had a huge recreational room, hot showers, a kitchen, as well as prepared dinners for an extra cost.

When I reached the campsite area, only about two soccer fields away, I was the first to arrive. It had a section of about 12 tent sites which perched above the basin. Most of the spots were on bare muddy ground which sloped towards the water. I examined all the sites, seeking to choose one I thought was the best. After consideration, I took a spot-on level grass overlooking the Loch. I spent the time to set-up my tent and unloaded my backpack. Afterwards, I returned to the Hostel for a shower and to prepare a meal on my own. Finally, I paused in the recreational area to charge my cell phone as I relaxed in the warmth. They filled it with all ages, including many school groups. As I read my guide, I remained silent. I penned in my journal and fought the desire to snooze. I resembled a youthful child bobbing his head, fighting the urge.

As a few hours passed, it was time to retire to my tent. Upon my return, there were about 10 to 12 tents set up around me. I climbed into my tent and bundled under my quilt. The harmony between wind and water was my background noise. I noted a significant cleansing in myself as I sank into the tranquil surroundings. I drifted off despite my excitement, knowing I was ascending Ben Lomond tomorrow.

I feel I have the courage to go after what I want out of life. I am charting my course and staying true to myself.

"Sometimes when you are in a dark place, you think it has buried you, but you have actually been planted."
—Christine Caine

"I am striving to gain a lesson from every experience and use my experiences as a steppingstone for development of self."
—Edgar Cayce

"Do not wait around for your life to happen to you. Find something that makes you happy and do it. Because everything else is all just background noise."
—George Mason

I continue to believe everything is possible. I am profoundly grateful for what I have.

CHAPTER 14

Comparable to my forty days on the Camino de Santiago, I had taken note my way of life had taken on a flawless straightforwardness once more. Time stopped having any meaning. When it was sunless, I retreated to bed. When the daylight rose and the light was adequate, I arose. Everything in between was simply, in between, savoring the occasion of the marvelous countryside. It was completely superb.

I had no commitments, burdens, or obligations, no exclusive desire, and, as it were, the littlest of wants. All I had to do, have the eagerness to persevere in my walk.[5]

When I walked, I felt a Zen mode. My brain remained silent, as my actions were automatically similar to breathing. I did not listen to music or anything. I refreshed my soul with the surrounding nature.

> *"I go to nature to be soothed and healed and to have my senses put in order."*
> —John Burroughs

My mindset was rapidly recaptured, my grin returned, and the brief cloud of pattern lifted. I knew I was upbeat. I was doing what I loved to do.

*"It's better to fail while striving for something wonderful,
challenging, adventurous, and uncertain, then to say,
'I don't want to try because I may not succeed completely.'"*
—Jimmy Carter

CHAPTER 15

BEN LOMOND

I had a new keenness and determination. I maintained my intention of savoring each step and the moment, and not rushing through the beauty of the West Highland Way. Ben Lomond was my destination.

As I awakened to a joyful new day under my tent shelter, I listened to the Loch below my tent, with its waves rolling onto shore. I unzipped my gateway to a splendid morning. Sitting outside of my shelter, perched on a log, was a small wood warbler in its luminous yellow and green feathers. It stunned me the bird allowed me to sit within a foot or less as he gazed upon me. It was as if we were sharing a conversation over tea.

I loaded up everything even though I was planning another night of encampment in the same location. I did not wish to leave my tent up and belongings while I would be gone all day. Plus, I was going to move myself to steeper ground as the night's forecast was for rainfall.

After eating breakfast and a hot shower, the Rowardennan Lodge Youth Hostel allowed me to stash my backpack in the rec room. I set up a lighter pack for the day's journey. I knew I did not wish to lug a heavy backpack over the terrain I would deal with. The daypack carried a bottle of water, my water filter, snacks, along with my camera gear.

I exited the Hostel to climb Ben Lomond. Ben Lomond was Scotland's most southerly Munro. The peak was 973 m, (3,195 feet). A striking detail was once one reached the summit, one had superb vantage viewpoints of Loch Lomond and a substantial portion of the West Highland Way.

According to the guidebook, "West Highland Way-Glasgow to Fort William," there were two route choices. In theory, they created a loop or, if preferred, one could ascend and descend by employing the same route. The most straightforward route, sadly less appealing, was the well-maintained path beginning opposite of the Ben Lomond Shelter near the car park. The course was before the Youth Hostel. The attractive alternative way ascended via the subsidiary summit of Ptarmigan before scaling the arduous north-west ridge to the top. They recommended it, with the added advice to bring a map and compass with you. Despite this, I concluded either track would be accurately marked, and other people would also be on the trails.

I chose the Ptarmigan Route. As I reached it, they carved it on a wooden marker constructed from a tree section divided in half. I discovered the trailhead after passing the Ben Lomond Cottage. It was a narrow trail on the right promptly after navigating a concrete bridge. To my surprise, there was a free encampment area there as well. After a few minutes upon the route, a waterfall appeared into view. Something had quite enamored me with waterfalls. It was overflowing rock steps which disappeared into the elevation of the forest.

After climbing a bracken-covered hillside, I had to move through a kissing gate. It opened the trail to steepening ground. As I expected, the pathway was well-worn and simple to adhere to. As the elevation occurred under my footsteps, I reconnected to the below waterfall as it flowed high above me, piercing through the conifer plantation. The views of Loch Lomond overtook me as the landscape zigzagged skyward. I halted many times to look over my shoulders and snap pictures of the Loch at different elevations. The panoramic views were stunning. The landscape offered the traditional Scotland high grass which occupied its vast pastureland. In the distance, it appeared boggy.

The blessing of the day was not being all alone. I could ask other trekkers to snap a picture of me throughout the hike. I noticed landscape pictures had an added charm when people were captured on film.

As the elevation rose, around 751 m, (2,398 feet), near the Ptarmigan ridge, the wind intensified in velocity along with a misty drizzle. At that moment, I had on my puffy jacket and my rain parka and Buff over my head and ears to lessen the chill.

As I neared Ben Lomond, it appeared to rise as a stairway to heaven.

> *"Good things await you on the other side of that ridge. That is a hill you can climb. Just put one foot in front of the other."*
> —Neale Donald Walsch

It was apparent at a glance I was entering a new realm of magnificence and challenge. The trail shifted into a rigorous, steep hiking jaunt. The rock steps to the summit were demanding at my five-foot six-inch frame. Luckily, I had my trekking poles to use as assist to support my balance as well as dig into the rock foundations to serve me an extra assistance to achieve the climb.

Despite the strenuous climb, I remained eager and excited. The entire trek was upon open territory under a dome of blue sky.

As I summited from the Ptarmigan Route, I felt a sense of triumph. Over four miles upward onto the summit with thirty plus miles per hour howling winds. I had views to every horizon, an experience not to be forgotten. The view from the top was gorgeously panoramic, though the gusting wind was intense. Mother nature was grinning upon me. I breathed out in a single enormous puff. At that point, stillness overtook me as I stared at the gigantic Scottish vista.[5]

I paused on the summit to have my lunch. On my excursions, I had a touch of affinity. I was exactly where I ought to be. I tried to locate a place out of those gusting winds, but it was challenging. The surface offered no objects to use as a windbreaker.

I enjoyed my lunch of pepperoni and cheese on crackers, along with a chocolate chip cookie for dessert. As I enjoyed my lunch, I reflected on how grateful I was for the experience. Although I had to return to civilization, beyond any doubt, I knew outings of that nature did not happen each day. I treasured each last drop.[9]

Upon descent, I chose the wide, easily angled tourist route. As I departed the summit and the miles ticked away, I could understand how that direction was deemed sluggish, uninspiring. The path provided mud along with puddles. I walked with the Loch on my horizon. The observation of that course was it seemed easier even if leading up in the same direction.

When I was summiting, a sizable group of individuals who all appeared to be above the age of 65 were descending the summit onto the Ptarmigan route. I watched their struggle, and a few almost fell because of the strenuous gradient and terrain. I contemplated the difficulty which remained ahead of them. As I experienced a steep climb, they had to deal with an arduous descent. I believed personally, a steep descent was more challenging and treacherous. I read previously, most people who perished climbing Mt. Everest are on the descent from the summit and not the ascension.

The descent presented no wildlife even though I was strolling through the pastureland of sheep and cows. I had to pass through another kissing gate. Overall, the route had many more leveling sections, which meant easier walking. As I concluded the trek of the day, I was thankful I chose the tough course.

I returned to the Hostel and paid for another night of camping. When I returned to the encampment area, I was third to set-up a tent for the evening. Sadly, the others had chosen the top two spots. I chose a different section upon higher ground, which was as flat as possible. I unpacked my belongings. It was the third night of camping for me, and I was still trying to improve my setting up each time. I wanted to assure my tent did not leak and allowed the most room as possible inside to avoid condensation issues.

After camp set-up, I returned to the Hostel and paid for their supper, chili-con-carne with bread. It was wonderful not having to worry about cooking. The dinner was hot and delightful. With the last morsel, I went to the recreational room. I spotted a space I could charge my devices and read from my guidebook about tomorrow's stage. Near me was a youthful gentleman. His name was Brandon, and it turned out he lived in the Bahamas and recently went through a hurricane. I revealed I lived on St. Croix of the US Virgin Islands and dealt with two back-to-back Category 5 Hurricanes. We chatted about what it was like during the time for both of us. I had to live three months with no electricity or clean running water as we reconstructed our island. He answered he had to go for roughly a month. He was taking off the next afternoon onto the next stage, past my expected ending point. Two other men, in their mid-60's, introduced themselves as well. It was entertaining sharing a conversation. I felt so blessed with what I had seen and done through my experiences. I could easily have overwhelmed the discussion to share them. However, I also sensed I appeared a tad narcissistic when I did. Instead, I fixated on the others and maintained my silence to listen to their narratives and their impressions about the West Highland Way so far.

Once my batteries charged to capacity, I extended my best wishes to the three gentlemen and retired to my tent. I assured my stakes and guidelines were taut as I climbed into the shelter. Lying supine embedded in my quilt, a tranquility overcame me.

During the night, the rainfall flowed, though not remarkably hard. Adequate water penetrated my tent at its peak on my right side. There was nothing I could do except attempt to transfer myself to the side where it was dry. Unfortunately, I dozed only briefly that night.

Turns out, I made two huge mistakes during my earlier set-up. First, I allowed my footprint to be outside my tent floor barrier. That mistake could create a pond or river under the tent and increase the chances of water coming through the thin tent floor material. My second mistake was I kept my side vestibules close to my tent. Being a single pane, the water passed through it. With every touch to the sides, water fell into my tent.

"It's a blessing for a man to have a hand in determining his own fate."
—Blackbeard

"Life can only be understood backwards, but we must live it forwards."
—Soren Kierkegaard

CHAPTER 16

ROWARDENNAN TO DOUNE BOTHY

Awakened to dripping water into my tent by the door from the apex where my walking stick provided support, I decided it was best to stay awake, though it was only 6:00 am. I researched the weather report and noticed heavier rain was predicted within the hour. The day promised wind and rain. I pressed to pack up my belongings and loaded up my backpack for the day's trek. Sadly, in my rush, I misplaced my $600 prescription glasses by leaving them behind. A dreadful mistake, which I detected later in the day when it was too late to return.

According to the guidebook, it turned out most people would strike off to Inversnaid or Inverarnan that day, an approximately 7-14-mile trek based on which city.

Instead, I was setting an intention for the Doune Bothy. No matter the destination, the day's walk would be a lovely, forested stroll along the shore of Loch Lomond. It was seven miles to the first major town of Inversnaid.

As invariably in the morning, I dressed first in a dry-fit t-shirt, a light-weight fleece, then my puffy jacket with my rain jacket in an outside compartment for a quick grab.

Within a brief distance from the Hostel, I reached a split of the trail. There was an easy, "high" route which continued on a forestry track, passing several waterfalls. A harder alternative route dipped down to the Loch on a narrow single tracked path. It forged a tortuous course, clinging as tight to the seashore as it dared. The path comprised many short, steep climbs, decayed trees, as well as rocky sections. The reward was the immersion in glorious oak woodlands with wonderful loch-side views.

I partook in the lower, more challenging path. It was narrow, primarily the width of one hiker. The trail was about two meters above the Loch to my left. To the right was dense green grass on sloping hillsides. I was embracing a new fondness for my environment.

As the steps clicked away, a sprinkle started falling. It generated an expansive silence, severed solely by my tiny grunts and labored breaths as I neared stoned steps, which occasionally were loftier than I could ordinarily climb, having to employ my trekking poles. The steepness caught me off guard on occasion. When passed by other adventurers because of their brisker pace, I would have to pause, standing sideways to grant their passage.

As the light rain ceased, I promptly discarded layers to my T-shirt to diminish the perspiration. Even though the day was in the mid-50's, I sensed a warmth over me it could be in the 90s.

As my miles disappeared, I passed many secluded beaches. I pondered how those would have been remarkable for wild camping experiences. Another vital lesson I continued to learn was the plethora of water. I had plentiful opportunities to refill my water supply because of the streams, creeks, and Lochs which provided fresh Scottish water.

Sadly, I saw no mammal wildlife. They recognized the region for the Red Deer species and Feral goats to be roaming the area. With the path along the Loch, I could check out ducks along with many bird species.

Along the trail, I paused to the west to see "The Cobbler," the summit of Ben Arthur of 884 meters, (2900 feet).

I was thankful I was wearing my waterproof socks. Because of the rain, many stream crossings, the trail runners were saturated. My feet were dry as a bone.

When I arrived at Inversnaid, I marveled at the spectacular waterfalls and rock pool viewable as one had to pass over a wooden bridge and descend a staircase into Inversnaid. I halted at the Inversnaid Hotel for lunch. Besides eating (cheeseburger and fries), I lulled for approximately an hour to recharge my phone and camera batteries. I inquired about the rate for the night. It converted to about $135. Overall, it was a welcoming place, established directly on the trail.

I spotted a free camping area about five minutes from the hotel built near a boathouse. It was a clearing of undulating high grass. I contemplated an evening there. But it excited me to reside in a Bothy for the night.

A major attraction I reached shortly after the hotel pause was Rob Roy's Cave. Rob Roy MacGregor, the Robin Hood of the Highlands, was born in 1671. After they declared Rob Roy an outlaw, he was on the run for over ten years. Though captured several times, he repeatedly managed an escape in daring ways. It boosted his image to the country. Eventually, he turned himself in. Ultimately, the king pardoned him. He passed away in peace at 63.

I chose not to see the cavern or its nooks and crannies. It had a concealed entrance down a steep trail. The guidebook described there was not much to see upon the arrival except the white graffiti lining the entrance, "CAVE." I spotted two abandoned packs on the trail. I assumed two trekkers had decided to explore the historical site.

I advanced on the Way along rugged paths, and every so often had to squeeze between boulders and trees occasionally. The landscapes offered rock-strewn, craggy ground through hazel, silver birch, and hawthorn forest. There were numerous opportunities to pause at beaches. I observed previous burned ground circles from earlier campsites, which was odd knowing fires were looked down upon.

Throughout the day, the rainfall intensified or dissolved. As I neared the Doune Bothy around 4:30 pm, it increased to its heaviest. The trail turned into a muddy mess. The Bothy was primitive and awesomely lovely. They directly constructed it on the route. Out front to the right of the trail was a bog of high grass and swampy appearing ground. There was a rushing stream outside, as well as a forest of trees to the right. Because of the volume of rainfall falling, the pathway was essentially a stream of mud itself.

As one entered onto the concrete floor, to the left against the rear wall was a raised wooden platform which stretched the full width of the Bothy. In the middle of the room was one round plastic table with four chairs. Against the back wall was a table where earlier hikers had donated equipment as well on the wall as per the rules. To the right of the entrance were two separated raised platformed slabs separated by a mid-sized open stoned fireplace.

On my platform, merely wide enough for me, I first spread out my plastic tent ground cover, then inflated the Neo-Air mattress, inflated my pillow, then draped the quilt overtop with my sleep liner prepared as well. I unloaded my entire backpack around me to allow everything to dry out and to repack in the AM.

At first, I was alone for about twenty minutes. Then two girls from Germany arrived. It was about 5:00 pm with two and a half hours of sunlight remaining. The underlying rule besides keeping the place as clean as achievable was to have kindling and wood for the next person to use. The previous occupants crammed the fireplace with damp leaves, twigs, large fragments of wood. I emptied the fireplace and reconstructed a smaller version. The paper I asked for was damp because of the air's humidity. I even tore up index cards, which I devoted an hour to with meditational phrases. After about 15-minutes of struggling, no flames. I spotted a leftover bottle of fuel stove on the donation table. I attached my stove and employed it as a torch. Sadly, even that did not remedy the situation. Disheartened, I gave up.

About twenty minutes thereafter, a couple from Germany with their three dogs arrived and took the platform to my right. The girls used the large platform in the Bothy's rear. After introductions, the husband removed dry Firestarter from his bag and used a new tampon of his companion's. After about ten minutes, he had the fire ablaze. I settled by the snapping blaze, tragically transmitting small warmth; I attempted to move in closer to the embers, but the concrete foundation would not allow it.[1]

Thereafter, even though raining, I ventured out into the nearby forest with him to gather as much fresh firewood as attainable, not solely for us, but to follow the rules for the next day.

As the rain continued to fall outside, and darkness reigned, newer and more individuals entered the Bothy. By the conclusion of the night, about twenty trekkers have found refuge here. The people were side by side on the rear platform, another half dozen on the concrete floor. Most of the languages were foreign to me. People prepared dinner on the plastic table with the front door open to allow ventilation. The overall aroma was stagnant and foul because of everybody entering being soaked from the outside downpour as well as the German couple with three dogs. There were stringed lines stretching throughout the Bothy to attach whatever needed to be dried. Tents, shirts, socks were draped around as curtains. By the end of the evening, everywhere there was stuff; tents, clothes, backpacks, rain covers; hanging out to dry. The floor by the door was filthy and wet. The exposed concrete floor was damp. The walls were uninsulated. I settled by a window with no draft. Ultimately, it was like camping in an old garage.

I shared a conversation primarily with the wife of the German couple to my right because of her speaking a lot more English than the husband. Unfortunately, I could not recall their names. They were over there to walk the Way as well. Because of the dogs, they were wild camping every night with over 200 pounds of gear. They had to carry the dog food, dog items, besides their equipment. She even mentioned they had to leave behind equipment at their departing hotel because they had packed too much.

In the background, chiefly German dialect was being spoken. Nevertheless, being alone, it was nice to listen to some voices.

Eventually, as the fire died down, the time around 11:00 pm, quiet stilled the night. Though silent, I could not fall asleep. I laid there listening to the dogs move around, others shifting positions on their air mattresses, along with the snoring, coughing. Another day of trekking, and I could not sleep.

When I arrived as the only one there, I thought perhaps it would remain that way. It surprised me with the amount of people who came in after dark in the rain. I wondered what time they started that day and what distance they have walked.

Around 2:00am, the rainfall has ceased, and I had to venture outside to use the restroom. I peered at the most remarkable full moon I have ever encountered, with white, fast-drifting clouds. I thought I had to capture it on video and photos. When I re-entered, all three dogs commenced to bark noisily, waking everybody up. On one side, I felt awful for making the dogs to bark, however, I likewise felt sad for the owners, because it was their dogs who woke up everyone. With that happening, I chose to lie back down and not try to return outside with my camera.

As I relaxed my body, my mind went into overdrive with thoughts. "I concluded I had a choice for how I am going to live my life. Each day, I advance forward with purpose. I have strength. Today, I am free."

"Your heart knows the way. Run in that direction."
—Rumi

CHAPTER 17

DOUNE BOTHY TO CRIANLARICH

Eventually, the dawn arrived. As others arose and commenced packing their damp belongings, I lingered under my quilt, listening. I delayed my departure, as most were gone. I then patiently took my time to collect my articles into their correct section of my 60-liter backpack. It felt like not a thing ever dried.

The precipitation was a memory as yesterday's gray tones were replaced with a morning sky of aquamarine and powdered with stark ivory clouds. Exiting the dwelling, the outside and the initial 100 yards of trail were a torrent of mud and water.

I was considering a shortened day, ending in Inverarnan, 10 kms, (about 6.5 miles). The first reason was the section had a reputation of being one of the toughest sections. Second, because of the poor night in the Bothy of tossing and turning, I was contemplating a shelter with heat as well as a lengthy hot shower.

The morning passed quietly as the trail passed underneath my LonePeaks slowly and unwaveringly. Approaching Ardleish, the route continued passable, but saturated with Scottish muck and water. The streams had transitioned into small rivers.

After passing Ardleish, I looked at my last views of Loch Lomond. I neared the Beinglas Farm. They deemed it an excellent location for the night as the Way passes it. It possessed an immense field for camping along with private huts which slept two people (allowed to rent solo). Wistfully, I entered too early. They were cleaning. I would have to wait around three hours before I could check in. Instead, I chose to move on to the next section.

The next area was about 10 km, (about 6.5 miles), Crianlarich. They regarded it as the halfway point of the West Highland Way. Overall, the section was pleasant and undemanding. The path turned to rough sheep pastures along with open hillsides. I paused for a snack by the River Falloch because of the impressive, appealing rapids.

A negative to the day's trek was the previously washed-away bridge. It occurred a month or so before I left the mainland of the USA. As I approached the detour, I spotted the washed-away bridge. I discovered the bridge on a temperamental river. Instead of a brief few steps to cross the bridge, I had to slough through a slippery, muddy uphill for a half-mile to another bridge crossing. Once across, the terrain yielded to a wide dirt track route.

My favorite aspect of the day was encountering grazing sheep and goats. I had one approach me and paused about a foot away. The sheep only had one horn, perhaps because of fighting. He was a pretty shade of white with a blackened face and white snout.

As I reached a marker for Crianlarich, a decision was to be made. I could walk one mile downhill into the township or remain on my course and discover a site to wild camp. I was fatigued, so I rested on a nearby bench between two pine trees to contemplate. With my shoulders unburdened from my pack, I thought about the pros and cons. As my breathing quietened from the pause, I strolled into town. I plotted to locate a bed-and-breakfast for the evening.

As I entered the township, I noticed every bed-and-breakfast had a no vacancy sign on it, which perplexed me, as it was mid-September. There was a hostel in town; nonetheless, I wished for privacy. Luckily, before giving up and returning to the skyward path, I tapped on a door of a bed-and-breakfast with no sign out front, The Craig Bank Guest House. It had one room available. She said the one room left would cost me like a double. The room only possessed one bed. I thought, is she doing this because she hopes I say no, or to take advantage of a tired hiker. By that time, I was ready to pay threefold if I had to for a bed and a hot shower. So, $65 for a small chamber by the street was my charge.

After checking in, unpacking, plus a long hot shower. I departed and went to the local tavern for a celebration feast. I had completed half of the West Highland Way. I relished my meal.

As I relaxed in the bed, I was thankful for another day of stunning views. I rejoiced on the path, thumping off the miles. I felt a subtle, essential something which made my environment satisfying. It was simple to proclaim over a panorama or appreciate nature in general as I went.5 I acknowledged being empty of thought, cheerily retained with the occupation of urging onward. Life was all about the journey.

"Embrace uncertainty. Some of the most beautiful chapters in our lives won't have a title until much later."
—Bob Goff

CHAPTER 18

CRIANLARICH TO TYNDRUM

I awoke in my heated accommodation with the aroma of an extravagant breakfast prepared by the proprietors. Once clothed, I shuffled into a stunning glass enclosed courtyard. The plate presentation was tantalizing with scrambled eggs, beans, pork, along with natural juices. The choices of pastries were appetizing as well. I savored each mouthful as I cleared my plate.

Unfortunately, upon returning to my chamber, I discovered I had the heat raised too high; it was like hitting a concrete wall. The room had taken on the stench of my tent, backpack, and other belongings. I acted swiftly and opened the windows, which did not have screens, to air out. Once I packed, I left the room with the door open to enhance the circulation. Disastrously, the owner's spouse entered the area moments after I departed it to snag the sheets and the towels. She made a negative criticism to me applying so much heat, inquiring why I had it so high and maintained it all night. I guess they typically reduce the heat at night in their residence. She declared how new people they expected today, and now the room may be unusable because of the stench. I instantaneously felt wrong and apologized for operating the heat at such a high rate. Her husband, on the other hand, understood my position and simply grinned and stated, "have a delightful day." I closed the main door and returned to the trail.

I returned the one-mile uphill to the juncture I was at the day before. After pausing at the halfway marker, I began the 10 km, (six mile), section towards Tyndrum. Practically instantly, because of the sustained climbing of altitude, the "Twin Peaks" of Ben More and Stob Binnein came visible. They recorded Ben More at 3,851 feet, and they recorded Stob Binnein at 3,821 feet in elevation.

The next two and a half miles were through an extensive conifer plantation high on the valley side. The trail descended to a horizontal valley floor which crossed the River Fillan and a circuitous route through farmland.

The charm was because of the open landscapes. There were repeatedly airy views of a real, lived-in world: sheep ranches, cottages, even an occasionally used railway track. It was challenging to not wish to pause and appreciate the exquisitely picturesque landscapes snapping picture after picture.

At that stage of the trip, I met hardly a soul. I might have counted five or seven other hikers who passed me.

A location which stood out to me was the Strathfillan Wigwams. It was an Auchtertyre Farm. It provided an immense field for tents, which had a benefit, a fire pit. The bunkhouses, lodges, along with yurts afforded privacy and enhanced comfort. Another positive feature was their farm market. The store comprised natural cheeses and produce. It was an excellent location for a night, but as well as a splendid stopping spot for a break along with a nutritious snack. While enjoying an apple from their private orchid, I reconnected with the German couple briefly and with their three dogs. I examined in amazement the volume of gear they had. He dragged a cart when able and she carried two backpacks. I noticed the cart could be worn as a backpack if desired during undulating terrain. Pondering for a moment, I recalled crossing paths with them between Balmaha to Rowardennan.

I was somewhat disappointed after I departed. I arrived in a region of the resident Scottish cows. These were reddish, with long shaggy coats, along with horns. My inner excitement brewed to see the new species of a cow I have never gazed upon. I approached a small fenced in section. There were three foraging, but all were on the ground, so I did not have a superb view of them because of the surrounding tall grass. It was the only moment of my journey of seeing those unique species of cow.

Before I departed for the West Highland Way, I read the book, "A Walk in the Woods," by Bill Bryson. I thought about him as I stepped through the timber of silver birch and rowan along with pine forests. Throughout his writing, he discussed his fondness for the trees on the Appalachian Trail.

A blessing of the West Highland Way was the easy access to water. Every few strides a trekker would cross a stream, walking by a Loch, or a river.

I reached Tyndrum about 2:00 pm. It was a village which had shifted into a popular stopping place for travelers. I stopped at the By the Way Hostel and Campground. It provided a modest grassy field for tents, the hostel, along with trekker huts. I spent the 25-euros on a hut. Inside were two twin beds, a heater, and shelter from the outside temperatures and rain. It had no bathroom or shower, which was about a football field elsewhere, where the laundry was, and a space where meals could be prepared.

The owner was a superb host. He was an avid trekker himself, especially after he closed in October. He presented me pictures of him mountain camping in the areas I was about to cross. I mentioned I was aiming to scale a few of the local peaks. After reviewing my ideas, he was quick to explain reality to me. The trails on those summits were not properly marked. He proposed I purchase a paper map and a compass. He cautioned me against my proposed side detour the next day without them. I was going to pursue the trip anyhow. However, the owner recounted a story of a young gentleman who stumbled and snapped his leg recently on the same trail. He had to crawl himself down for help. He added if I was dead set on my idea, I could go over to the outdoor equipment store across the street and see if they had a map of the territory.

Because of my earlier leaky night in my tent. I set-up the tent in front of my hut. It was calling for rain overnight and I wanted to see if it would leak. I wished to also purchase some sort of waterproof spray to apply.

I unpacked my belongings and ventured to the district which had the stores and restaurants. The noteworthy feature about the area was the sign reading no further stores for roughly 40 kilometers, to Kinlochleven, as the West Highland Way would enter the remote parts.

The one belief of which I had taken note, I had not in any way yearned for my homeland or had wistfulness. I had grasped the autonomous way of life, of self-discovery and travels, of doing difficult things and composing the experiences, of bucking the framework and being wild. When I was on my treks, I was in my perfect world, abundantly grateful.[5]

I wished for a true home. However, I would consistently yearn to spend one or more months shouldering a backpack some place in the world and sharing it to my readers, desiring to create inspiration along with value. I believed life was full of exciting things to explore and understand.

*"The dark night of the soul is a journey into light,
a journey from your darkness into the strength
and hidden resources of your soul."*
—Caroline Myss

CHAPTER 19

TYNDRUM TO INVERONRAN

I woke up from a reasonable night's sleep. The radiator inside the hut was loud, so I merely ran it as necessary. I did not want to disturb my next-door neighbor as the huts shared a common wall. I learned quickly most people I had met throughout my experience in Scotland discontinued their heat at night.

Once packed, I checked on my tent. The rain came as promised, as it saturated the exterior with left over rain pellets. It pleasantly surprised me observing the interior of my tent was completely dry. After the tent was rolled up and placed into its proper exterior pocket. I walked over to the mini grocery store at the Green Welly petrol station to add a few extra supplies and to snag a sandwich to carry with me for lunch.

I departed the Tyndrum village and headed off. A small sign stated over 40 kilometers (24.9 miles) to the next town/city for re-supply, Kinlochleven. Yet I noticed quickly that was not absolutely correct. Many times, a small store or restaurant was present to collect food or snacks etc. Bridge of Orchy, a popular destination site, was about 11 kilometers (seven miles), away.

The track began mostly on level ground along the worn cobbled surface of an old military road. Mountain scenery enveloped it. Soon, I had a remarkable view of Beinn Dorain (elevation of 1076 m/3529 ft). Next to me, most of the day, was a railway. It was mentioned the railway was active, but seldom utilized.

The early afternoon unfolded when I entered a patch of steep descending slopes. I spotted a great rock to have a break and devoured my sandwich. I peered off into the horizon. Not a cloud in the sky. A few trekkers strolled by. Other than that, it was a silent day on the Way. I paused for about a half hour, soaking up the scenery. Wonderfully, the sandwich I purchased was yummy.

As the break concluded, I returned to my clay track.

A sad normal for me. After I eat, my stomach can relay signals, and I demand a bathroom break quickly. Luckily, as the pressure formed in my tummy and gas escaped my body, I was near the Bridge of Orchy. The negative to the West Highland Way up to that time was the minimal privacy. Thus, it was challenging to go off the trail if one required a bathroom. I have heard women had to become creative in order to diminish their vulnerability. Once in a while, one may come across a large boulder. But there were minimal woodlands like the Appalachian Trail. On the outskirts of Bridge of Orchy, I was astounded to see a train station, then sadly, a sign declared no restrooms. I had to endure another mile to the Bridge of Orchy Hotel. Prayers arose not to have an infant's accident. Each passing gas was a dread of losing my shit.

Bridge of Orchy was a tranquil hamlet. Surrounding it were the dramatic slopes of Beinn an Dothaidh and Beinn Dorain. I elected to stop at the Hotel not solely for a bathroom break, but a hot meal as well. Patiently awaiting of the delivery of hot fries and a Turkey sandwich, I read in my guidebook there was a free popular campsite across an elegant 18th-century bridge over the river about a quarter of a mile further north.

Originally, I plotted to remain there for two full nights. I was going to ascend Beinn Dorain and Beinn an Dothaidh on a side day trip. They deemed it a moderately strenuous climb, which might take up to or over seven hours. It was best to be an accomplished hillwalker. They suggested having a map along with a compass as well. The route offered low visibility on occasion. There were tales of individuals wandering onto the steep ground on the western border of the mountain and falling to their death.

As I neared the field, I noticed a few tents occupying the space. Instead, I proceeded on. I spoke to myself, "I will walk until I considered myself fatigued and would wild camp." The next township of Inveroran was another five kilometers (3 miles) away.

Instantly leaving the Bridge of Orchy, the terrain became challenging. Yet the superb landscapes formed an open trek I would cherish. They regarded it as the remotest and wildest section of the whole Way, because of no escape routes or shelters for the next 16-kilometers, (10 miles).

At one moment, I was at an altitude of 320 meters (1050 feet). It brought me above the timberline, which formed exquisitely beautiful open countryside. I could look at outstanding views over Loch Tulla, Rannoch Moor, as well as the Black Mount. I reflected, "I was in harmony, and I realized I walked in loveliness."[1]

As I arrived at the township of Inveroran, I paused at their hotel for a quick bathroom break along with double checking my guidebook for the position of the established wild encampment area. On the map, it appeared closer than it was in reality. It expressed it was 400 meters away. I expected I would see tents easily. The hotel had a Walker's Bar offering discounted meals for trekkers. Instead of a last supper or a cold IPA, I took off walking away from the hotel until it disappeared. After crossing a bridge, the wild free campsite appeared.

It was a modest, undulated field next to a stream. It was part of the grazing territory of cattle, which were on the other side of the road.

I originally pitched my tent on a patch of lower flat ground, about ten yards from the bank of the stream.

After I set up everything, I talked with a gentleman I had seen a few times at various places along the Way.

His name was Benjamin. The man was in his 50s. He was from a small country in Europe. It began with the letter "C," yet I could not identify it on a map as I forgot the name by the time of this writing. He was a charming man. He owned the tent I had wished to purchase, though it was sold out. He walked with a single walking stick and a minor hitch because of an impaired knee. I observed his backpack. It was a quarter of the capacity of most trekkers I encountered. It seemed most European hikers had backpacks which were 75-liters or larger. Mine was a 60-liter, while his was a 48-liter.

I relocated my tent adjacent to him as the ground was higher and farther away from the passing stream. I hoped it would cut down the condensation on my tent.

As the sun began to set over the horizon, I prepared my couscous dinner using the camping stove. I learned from my previous lesson not to keep the steel wool near the flame.

The positive about the West Highland Way was the wealth of water. Regardless, I would filter it for safety. As I ate with my metal spoon, I dined in silence, peering out over the scenery. All that beauty launched an air of serenity.

The metal spoon produced an eerie tone as I grasped for the hot meal. I compelled myself to swallow the mix. I concluded I needed other camping meals, as the couscous did not tantalize my taste buds. I contemplated if performing a lengthy trek in America like the AT, I would have many more diverse choices at the grocery store than I did when I departed Glasgow. There was only a resident market near my hotel with limited tasty options.

Relaxing after my half-eaten dinner, I noticed about ten other tents distributed over the small pasture. A few about 25 yards away built a modest fire which danced in the breeze. A cow was about ten feet away, free grazing on the grassy pasture as his or her colleagues remained on the other side of the path.

As I lay there in the darkness of my tent, I reveled in the earth's bouquet. One could hear others snore, talk in their sleep, or change positions on their sleeping pads. The small river provided ambience to overshadow most of those noises. I placed headphones to diminish the remaining sounds, as I had nothing to help me sleep from a medication point of view. At times, it was disheartening not being able to sleep, especially after a full day of walking with my backpack in tow. However, I beamed with admiration. I hence closed my eyes ruminating, "what a heavenly day." 1 I asked for strength to endure along my journey.

"Wherever you are, be there. Lifestyle is not something we do; it is something we experience. And until we learn to be there, we will never master the art of living well."
—Jim Rohn

"Don't let your fear paralyze you. The scariest paths often lead to the most exciting places."
—Lori Deschene

CHAPTER 20

INVERORAN TO KINGHOUSE

I unzipped my tent to a misty morning with a modest chill. Most of the other campers had already taken off. I deliberated returning to the Inveroran Hotel for a hot breakfast and the use of their restroom. Instead, I chose my typical breakfast of a porridge bar and cashews. I said adieu to the neighboring cows and departed.

It blessed me as I entered on a broad track after passing over a Victoria bridge providing access to the River Abhainn Shira. The trail passed a stretch of sycamores, Scot pines, along with silver birch and alders. The bonus was the course was elevated above them, which I believed for the first time, an area an individual could disappear, thankfully. I had a demand for a potty break. I descended into the mini forest and found a secret section for my number two business. After I buried the cat hole, I returned to the route and advanced.

As the path expanded to extensive landscapes, the combination of mist, clouds and a breaking sunlight formed a glorious rainbow. It appeared to rise from the ground and finish into a space you could see terminate. Sadly, I saw no pot of gold. To add to its serenity, the Coire Ba, which was the grandest mountain amphitheater in Scotland, cradled the stunning hilltops of the Black Mount Deer Forest, ascending to a height of 1108 meters, (3,634 feet) at the summit of Meall a' Bhuiridh on the northern rim.[2]

The day went on as the trail flattened. I was absolutely in the Scottish Highlands with untamed scenery, uninhabited, and soddened. The fog hovered over the summits of the various passing mountains. A few times I saw if the mist would clear to grant a clear visual. Many opportunities allowed grand views over the Rannoch Moor. They considered it the largest uninhabited wilderness in Britain.

When I arrived at the River Ba, crossing over the Ba Bridge, I wavered for a snack break as I inhaled in the crisp Scottish air and offered thanks. Upon completion of my swift snack, I heaved my backpack and moved forward. A short time later, the pathway rose consistently towards the edge on the horizon.

The day's course topped out at 445 m (1,460 feet). After the summit climb, I descended gently towards Glen Coe.

The distant Kinghouse came into play. Upon the descent, I could have stayed at the Glencoe Ski Centre/Mountain Resort. It offered camping, micro lodges, along with a café. My initial idea was to have a zero day the following day in an adjacent city of Glen Coe. The Kinghouse Hotel/Bunkhouse was another one to two miles further down my path. The bus to Glen Coe stopped at the main road by the highway across the street from the hotel.

When I entered the outskirts of the King House Hotel, I spotted a building providing free bathrooms to trekkers. I pondered locating their free camping space. It was approximately a quarter mile on the other side of the hotel, across a small bridge and stream. Instead, I resolved a warm bed along with a hot shower would be better. When I inquired about a room in the hotel, it was $175 per night. Luckily, there was a bed available in the Bunkhouse. For $35, it was a clean room with four beds. At the moment, only one other young gentleman from Germany was in there. It afforded a shower, laundry accommodations, along with warmth as I slumbered. A choice to eat in the bar or the upper scale restaurant was the food choice. A positive to nature lovers, many dominical deer would graze out front on the roped off lawn.

After preparing my bunk along with a balmy shower, I conducted my first trip over to the bar restaurant. I ordered a cheeseburger with fries and a twist. Commonly, the burger was topped with Haggis. Since I was skeptical, I had the Haggis on the side. It was oval, dry, and appeared like a sausage patty. After devouring my burger and a pint, I cut into the Haggis patty. It stunned and shocked me at the remarkable taste, similar to spicy sausage. Advancing forward, I was a Haggis fan.

I returned to my chamber for a nap. I shared a conversation with my roommate. He was here for an abbreviated trip with a few classmates on their holiday from school. Without overpowering the discussion, we primarily chatted about my reasons for the trip, my burning ambition to create Tommy Ray Entertainment. I shared lessons I had learned, like life was fragile. Follow your heart with unwavering faith, as well as patience and perseverance. He said I was an inspiration. A sensation of warmth of gratitude saturated my soul as I slipped off to a nap.

I awakened as two new roommates appeared. A father and daughter entered. She was an avid trekker and finally talked her father into coming on a trip with her. I shared supper with him later in the evening.

At dinner, I began a conversation with a gentleman at an adjacent table. He had recently completed the Camino de Santiago. We shared a beer and dessert as we rehashed our memories of the Camino.

I enjoyed thinking I was impacting the world with my trip as well. Besides a personal journey, I liked to think I was creating inspiration and value to prove anything was possible.

"I cannot express how important it is to believe that taking one tiny, and possibly very uncomfortable step at a time can ultimately add up to a great distance."
—Tig Notaro

CHAPTER 21

KING HOUSE TO WILD CAMP

I awakened from slumber in my bed. It was a cozy, quiet night, despite having three roommates. I rolled out of bed into a hot, refreshing shower. I made my course over to the bar's restaurant for breakfast. It was a pre-prepared plate of Haggis, fried egg, pork, beans, and disc bread comparable to a crepe. The one negative of the experience, the breakfast was not worth the cost of 12-euros. I sat with my roommate from Germany and his friends and shared most of it with them. Upon returning to the room, I collected my belongings and left on the day's outing.

I nixed the original intention to visit Glen Coe for the day. I changed my mind to carry out the 9-mile side trip by the Citylink bus. Instead, I returned to the West Highland Way.

The day's test was the Devil's Staircase. They regarded the summit as the steepest point along the West Highland Way at 548 meters, (1,797 feet). It afforded magnificent views north to the Mamores with Ben Nevis rising behind.

I exited the bunkhouse and started towards Kinlochleven, a 14 km, (8.5 mile) trek. A few paces along the trail revealed an option of two routes. I could either choose a high route, which presented a safe route above the main road. It would be quicker and easier. Or I could advance along a "hidden trail" which would be slow, boggy, and tiring. I elected to travel high upon the rugged stone track. The lower trail was unpassable the day I saw it.

When I arrived at the base of "The Devil's Staircase," I observed a path laden with switchbacks rising 850 feet. It was extremely exposed. Luckily, the day was occupied with sparking sunshine along with indigo skies, which warmed my skin in dry warmth. Soldiers have been ascending that stone staircase since the 1750s. It was a sustained climb. The section was the busiest I had witnessed in my days on the West Highland Way. I estimated there were over 50 trekkers gradually making their move upwards.

Once over the summit, the trail began a gentle, long descent to the sea level in Kinlochleven. Before leaving, I gazed off into my surroundings. It awarded me far-reaching views of an unscathed vista.

During the descent, the pathway contoured across the mountainside and miles of wilderness to the east. Sadly, no wildlife was observed.

An unusual sight outside of Kinlochleven were long black water pipes leading from their township's generator. They were constructed to resemble a rollercoaster ride. They undulated with the landscape.

Overall, it was a spectacular day of walking across inspiring mountainous terrain. I paused in Kinlochleven, an industry village. Most claim it's ugly. An intriguing feature of the city was when I entered the downtown. The Ice Factor, an indoor climbing facility, was sponsoring some type of international event or competition. There were booths and sponsors crowding the parking lot around the facility.

Originally, I was planning to pause there for the night. I first stopped at a local grocery store for the essential supplies I liked to always carry, snacks and breakfast items. I then stopped at the MacDonald Hotel for a late hot lunch. They offered a tent camping ground, sadly the cost was 20 euros. I decided I preferred to search for a wild camping area along the trail.

I exited the MacDonald restaurant and ventured into a patch of birch woods. The trail zigzagged upwards. I thought maybe I made a mistake as the path was difficult. Yet like most strenuous activities, it provided stunning views of the Loch.

I emerged on a high bluff above the timberline. It

extended a long, sensational, unobstructed views all around me. The sun was mid-sky and falling.

Eventually, I was blessed to locate the precise spot I wished. It had a stream, excellent views, a pre-formed fire pit and bench. The negative was the higher temperature, the midges were buzzing all around. I had to put on my head net to block them from devouring me. I did my best each moment I opened my tent zipper to prevent any undesirable visitors.

As the sun was setting, I was alone. The town I left was four miles behind me and the next township was another seven to ten miles to go.

Sadly, because of the moisture in the air, combined with the preceding days of rain, no matter what I tried, I could not ignite the timber. I wished I had known what I discovered in hindsight, that I was only going to walk a few hours after the preceding town. I should have acquired Firestarter like the "log" or kenneling. I purchased cotton facial pads, thinking it would be adequate. Unfortunately, nothing but a whiff of white smoke.

I prepared supper using my camp stove. In the distance was Beinn A' Bheithir, "the hill of the thunderbolt," (1024 m, 3359 feet). With each bite, I savored the heavens vaulted above me, garnished with the stars.

I entered my tent; I recognized my travels were finishing. A night alone among the rustling stream, swaddled in darkness, listening with involuntary keenness for the telltale snap of a branch or stick.

As I laid upon the Neo-air, I mulled over how life progressed easily when I was on my undertakings. I yearned to persist, traveling through astonishingly exotic places. I perpetually walked and hiked to chase wonderment.[5]

I had allotted three weeks for my trekking on the West Highland Way. Though, once in Fort William, I was going to investigate if I could also add the Great Glen Way, another 75 miles.

*"Don't be pushed around by the fears in your mind.
Be led by the dreams in your heart."*
—Roy T. Bennett

*"Life moves pretty fast. If you don't stop and look
around once in a while, you could miss it."*
—Ferris Bueller

CHAPTER 22

WILD CAMPING TO GLEN NEVIS

The dawning appearance merged my world to color. I inched myself from the tent. The scenery cleared my haziness.[1]

I was excited to begin the final arduous trek to Glen Nevis. They declared it to be rewarding as it passed over beautiful high passes, then undulated through forests. Glen Nevis was about three miles shy of Fort William. The reason to spend two nights there was to ascend Ben Nevis, the highest peak in the neighboring countries.

The day commenced well under blue skies. Within one to two miles, I reached a section of buildings, practically all remnants/relics which were forged from jagged stones.

Surprisingly, the day turned summery and remained tranquil. It probably was in the low 70s with continuous sunshine with full exposure as one walked. A spectacular view greeted me. The toothy ridge of Aonach Ragach due south was marvelous.

After crossing into an open moorland, I could see stunning views to the north, which included Ben Nevis. It delighted me knowing I would be on its summit the next day. I proceeded, enchanted by the scale of the countryside. I was off in my own world.

As the day progressed and each sluggish mile unraveled. The isolation felt like having the entire nation of Scotland, or at least the West Highland Way to yours truly. I thought to myself, "as I trekked, it was simple for me to drop my look to the trail." "I never truly thought of the ceaseless movement, not noting the miles which vanished beneath my feet."

I considered amid those minutes, most of my journey was alone. Grasping the calmness of the solitude it rendered. Generally, I found myself wanting to walk alone. Maybe not fantastic for a travel essay. Be that as it may, I accepted I might accomplish moments of significant reflection. I was learning who I was at my inward essence. A tranquility immersed my consciousness. An expanded mindfulness took over my body.[5] The solidarity created serenity. I metamorphosed into an invisible energy. I was truly free.

> *"I love to be alone. I never found the companion that was so companionable as solitude."*
> —Henry David Thoreau

Sadly, near the end of the day, I trekked through what appeared to me as recklessness annihilation of a wooded forest. Stumps were beyond a countable quantity. I am sure they were needed; I would have preferred to witness the landscape laden with the grace of those trees.

Originally, I had proposed a quick side detour which stated about an extra 15 minutes of walking to observe the Dun Deardail or Iron Age Hill Fort. Besides remnants of the fort, striking close-up views of Ben Nevis were offered.

Unfortunately, as I reached the detour, my fatigue was too great to try. Perhaps the surprise of the day's heat or, simply worse, I quit on myself. I continued on the path to Glen Nevis. I allowed the inner coward to win. As I progressed a mile or so past, I hung my head in shame for the choice.

Eventually, I arrived at the Glen Nevis campground. After purchasing two nights of tent camping. I studied the map provided to display tent placement options. The first two locations, near the store, the laundry, and restrooms, were filling up and most tents had hardly six or fewer feet from another tent. I sauntered to the farthest field and noticed only a handful of tents pitched. I set up near a protected conifer tree by a tranquil stream in a level, grassy clearing. There was a nearby picnic table and a wooden fence as well. The closest tent to mine was over a football field away.

After performing laundry, I took a lengthy hot shower in the outstanding facilities. Instead of preparing my own food, I wandered to the nearby restaurant, the Glen Nevis Restaurant and Lounge Bar, for supper. I devoured a plate of fish and chips, along with a pint of beer. I recharged my phone along with reviewing my emails, Facebook, Twitter, as well as Instagram.

Upon my return, the heavenly skies had darkened. The temperatures had raised over the prior few days. It was cool enough not to sweat, but I did not have to use my quilt for warmth. I merely slipped into it about halfway. Throughout the night, I tossed and turned. I periodically double checked my feet to assure I was not against the single pane to collect condensation.

Finally, though, like most nights. I drifted off into a tranquil slumber.

"Good things await you on the other side of this ridge. This is a hill you can climb. Just put one foot in front of the other."
—Neale Donald

CHAPTER 23

ASCENDING BEN NEVIS

"You remember your first mountain in much the same way you remember having your first sexual experience, except that climbing doesn't make as much mess and you don't cry for a week if Ben Nevis forgets to phone you the next morning."
—Muriel Gray

They considered Ben Nevis the highest climbable summit in all of Britain. They recognized it to be remarkably beautiful. I was eager to see it at last. To achieve the summit of 1,344 meters (4,406 feet), I understood not to underestimate the effort required.

Daybreak emerged under a blazing blue sky. That day, I sensed Mother nature would be smiling upon me. I don't know if I was truly fatigued, or merely weakened from the stirring frenzy which comes from a long-anticipated launch.[1]

As I took off for the almost 14-mile round trip at 9:00 am, I was looking forward to what I wished would be a climactic amble. I dressed in my t-shirt, fleece pull-over with my tights and shorts. As I advanced in elevation, I assumed the temperatures would fall. I had a day backpack with my lunch, water, along with my rain jacket and gloves.

From my launching point at the Glen Nevis Campground, there were two choices. First, walk roughly three quarters of a mile towards the Visitor Center to the West and begin or walk about a half-mile east and take off at the Youth Hostel. The negative of the Youth Hostel was the first one mile was completely straight up compared to a steady incline from the Visitor Center.

I first began toward the Visitor Center. However, after walking roughly thirty minutes, I was troubled. Was I traveling in the incorrect direction? Or misinformed by the guidebook of the distance. Instead of entrusting the guidebook, I turned around and strode to the Youth Hostel where I was confident it began.

I crossed over a wooden footbridge aloft of the River Nevis to arrive at the beginning of the Youth Hostel trailhead. According to the posted sign, I was in for a roughly seven-mile expedition, all climbing skyward. With my pace, it would take me about four to five hours to summit.

The dreaded arduous trail to start me took 45-minutes in order to arrive at the actual Ben Nevis trail where it crisscrossed with the path from the Visitor Center. Because of the steep ascending, I was already dragging in my lower limbs. I halted at least twice on the steep climb to capture my breath and directed my throbbing legs to continue ascending. I met an older couple in their 60s taking my pathway as well. When they reached the top, luckily, there was a bench for a weary hiker. The gentleman was panting like a Saint Bernard.

Like always, as I carried out the original climb upon steep rock, I shedder layers promptly to my t-shirt alone. I was going to remove my tights as well. Yet, with others around me and no privacy, I kept them, even though they were originally uncomfortable because of the heat and stickiness from perspiration.

Ben Nevis was an imposing presence, a stony mass which rose from my starting position at the Youth Hostel. The mountain careened skyward at a jagged angle. It was a compelling sight.

Most of the route was single file or taking a risk on the slippery rocks to pass slower hikers. Sadly, on that day, I was encircled by at least a hundred hikers seeking the same deed. I spotted numerous sizable groups of students, along with other populous groups of people (many with identical t-shirts, climbing for a charity). Most advanced quicker than I, which was normal. I attempted to pass many myself on the treacherous single path laden with slippery dry rock.

The Tourist Route path was well maintained. The route was the most beloved. Ponies carrying supplies originally created it. At first, it ascended gently across the border of Meal an t-Suidhe.2 However, steep enough to me, it was an obsessive torture. There were three narrow bridges in the beginning which only supported one individual at a time, so people coming home had to wait or vice versa. At moments, the path felt seemingly endless. Of course, worth the endeavor. The path was a relentless slog of zigzags.

As the day progressed, I followed the route into the ravine established by the Allt na h-Urchaire, (Red Burn) which dropped off the western flanks of the Ben. As I gained elevation, I entered an expansive grassy pass on which Lochan Meall an t-Suidhe sits.[2]

About two hours into my journey, I considered a detour onto the Carn Mor Dearg Arete Route. They deemed it a superb route, nevertheless, tough, lengthier than the Tourist Route. I read it could add a few further hours to the trip to the summit. It frightened me I may not have sufficient time with my hiking pace to accomplish. I bypassed it and continued on the Tourist Route.

As I proceeded, the trail doubled back on itself, and I ascended across the western slopes. The route went by a waterfall which would mark perhaps a pause on the way home to refill my water bottle. When I was hiking, I always tried to drink from the surrounding natural resources, after I filtered the water. It generated a sensation inside of me that the location will always be a part of me. Once again, the zigzags returned as I ascended.

As I progressed, a view of Carn Dearg, (1221 m/4005 ft), was on my left. Eventually, I passed over a rock band as I came near the summit plateau.

I recall reading how Jim Davidson summed an ascension, "As I trudged along the path, I reflected the harshest part was coming to terms with the endless, dispiriting discovery there were always more hills. The point about being on a hill, as opposed to standing back from it, was one could almost never see precisely what was to develop. Each time one hauled oneself into plodding weariness, one gradually lost track of how far one had come. One believed one must surely approach the crest; one found there was in fact more hill beyond, sloped at an angle which blocked it from view before, and beyond that slope there was another, and beyond that another and another. Eventually, one reached a height where one could see, which enhanced one's spirit, though some may feel it was a pitiless deception. The elusive summit continually retreated by whatever distance one pressed forward, so each moment a view appeared, it dismayed one to see further climbing. Nevertheless, one staggered on. What else could one do? After one climactically reached the high ground, the summit, one was, oh, past caring. One basically wanted to find something to sit down on, eliminate the strain of one's rucksack, and contemplate. With an exhausted puff, one saw the view as electrifying. A tremendous backdrop."

One observation which formed a sense of sorrow was many individuals brought their dogs along on the trip. Please understand, the loose gravel was not the type one may encounter in one's driveway or buy at Home Depot to put in one's home garden. Those rocks were jagged and sharp. The bigger breeds, maybe I could understand, but many people had their small toy dogs with them. I could only image the pain and probably bloody paws they had at their completion.

I accomplished many zigzags, never ending miniature summits, until finally I saw my destination. After I summited, I inhaled deeply and was astounded at the wondrous views. A vivid turquoise sky, saturated with clouds, hovering above me. Typically, 300 days a year, a veil of clouds engulfs the area, causing views of a football field or two. Yet, on my day, I could see into another country. The land expanded out like a random-patterned quilt. The province below me loomed deserted.

The line to have one's picture captured with the summit's concrete marker by the kindness of another traveler was a wait of about 20 minutes. Though with patience, I had my picture snapped. After my picture, I paid it forward by aiding the hikers behind me. After completing my special moment, I ventured into a secluded area for my lunch. That became a laborious task. I had to venture over the volcanic-looking surface. The plateau was broad. All the same, one had to be careful; the plateau dropped precipitously into the Coire Leis below on the north side and into the notorious Five Finger Gully on the west side. In low visibility, there had been a handful of deaths where a walker simply took one too many steps and plunged to their demise.

To locate a position out of the gusting winds, (the winds were blowing at least 25-mph or greater. It chilled the air where once again I had to break out my puffy jacket to remain warm), to enjoy lunch as well to escape the trappings of the modern world around me. Sounds of cell phone conversations and the pervading stink of cigarette smoke reduced the options of the extensive plateau. After locating a spot using the stones for wind protection and assuring, I did not encroach on the tremendous drop off. I savored my sandwich; I had an appreciative gaze over the distant landscapes and lochs. A profound fulfillment cleared through me. I felt all the bliss and experienced a sense of amazement. I remained calm, profoundly moved, and absent in thought. I used the moment to rest and prepare for the approximately seven-mile descent to my tent.

Though off-limits, there was a primitive shelter on the peak adopted as an emergency dwelling/safety in case of dangerous weather and observatory ruins. I spotted some people attempted to scale the walls even though of the posted Do Not Climb signs were abundantly clear.

The descent provided a plethora of picture opportunities as I was seeing the same landscapes from a different viewpoint. Another positive, it seemed, fewer people were along the trail going down, perhaps because I had paused for over an hour on the summit plateau, cherishing the experience. Gazing off into the grassy lands of Scotland and with the distant undulating mountains, it constituted an enjoyable atmosphere. I stared off toward the skyline, saying, "thank you for my independence." I saw myself as courageous. The transparent blue skies with limited clouds allowed my eyes to see distant landscapes most would miss because of the routine Scottish cloud coverage. I was profoundly grateful for the day.

The descent, as one can imagine, took half the time. Though I must declare, I was not a fan of traveling downhill. With the combination of the steepness and loose rocks, it was easy to stumble. Luckily, my trekking poles bearded the weight to mitigate the pressure on my knees and caught me a handful of times from falling to the ground. A negative to my LonePeaks were though I considered them in the newness state, they offered minimal traction to other options afforded.

Back at the campground, besides the sensation of being blessed, I took a lengthy shower and returned to the walkable restaurant to enjoy dinner, a beer, and to update the world on my day's exploration. The next day I would complete the West Highland Way and find myself in a hotel bed for two to three nights, depending on my spontaneous next step. Later that night, it saturated me with a sense of openness, curiosity, and joy towards life. Every day was an exciting opportunity. Staring into my sheltered peaked roof, I told myself, "while I had life and strength, I would never cease from pursuing my daydreams, goals, and ambitions. I would not alter my ways, not even if I had to perish many times." Eventually, I lulled myself to sleep, inquisitive about what else was out there.

"Trust yourself. You have survived a lot, and you will survive whatever is coming."
—Robert Tew

"Making a big life change is scary, but you know what was even scarier? Regret!"
—Zig Ziglar

"I learned that courage was not the absence of fear, but the triumph over it. The brave man is not he who does not feel afraid, but he who conquers that fear."
—Nelson Mandela

CHAPTER 24

GLEN NEVIS TO FORT WILLIAM

The morning appeared, launching my day. The expanding daylight altered the blackened clouds toward lighter canopies of gray.[1] Pondering the last few miles, I was eager to see Fort William. I knew over the horizon there would be the termination of the West Highland Way. I had a slight homestretch perkiness in my steps. Although I had chosen not to fixate on the destination, as I was advancing closer, I craved to embrace the gratitude of the odyssey. The jaunt was what mattered.[5]

After leaving the campground, I paused along the early part of the trail to observe the Wishing Stone. They likewise considered it the Counsel Stone. It was an erratic boulder established to commemorate the victory of a Highland Chieftain. Though I preferred the legend behind the stone. It had the power to advise or counsel. Apparently, it could revolve. If one detected it in the act, one would discover the answers to three questions asked before it came to rest. Sadly, it was not rotating.

Blissfully, I did not have to walk by the main highway, the A82, the entire way into Fort William. There were two alternative options to maintain natural pathways, the "Peat Track" option, along with the "Around Cow Hill" option. I preferred those wooden paths which meant up and down hills, yet it was my last grasp of the wilderness before city life took over for a couple of nights.

I forked from the A82 to enter the Braveheart car park parking lot. I climbed steeply upon the "Around the Hill" option. After a brief plateau, I crested Cow Hill and, by "Douglas Place" stunning views of Loch Linnhe and my first visions of Fort William surfaced.

The weather stated the day to be pleasant with blue skies. However, one mile outside of Fort William, the rain commenced. The beads dribbled down the collar of my shirt, winding their way across my chest and back. The intensity strengthened as I paused for shelter under a canopy of trees. As the downpour returned to a mist, I advanced on the Way.

As the distance remaining came ever closer to zero, I guaranteed I did not peer past what was before me. I accepted it warranted my full consideration and appreciation. Right at that moment was the sole time I would ever have, which was a great thing.[7]

As the surroundings transcended from a wooded section to city life, delight arose inside me like a balloon keened to explode. I had an internal voice telling me I was almost at the ultimate resting place. I entered those city streets on the quest for the official end of the West Highland Way, a simple park bench with a sitting statue. It was at the end of High Street, a pedestrian only path laden with gift shops saturated with West Highland Way memorabilia. Blissfully, the rain halted as the end was in view. I arrived at the same time as a husband and wife. To aid the occasion, I first took pictures of them laughing and smiling next to the sculpture, then vice versa for our forever keepsakes. I inquired about where they were staying. Sadly, based on the observation upon entering Fort William, all the bed-and-breakfasts were filled. The bed-and-breakfast was my original choice owing to the splendid morning treats they provided in Scotland. The couple said they were at the Premier Inn near the train station, a destination for me in a couple of days. They claimed it was nice and economical. After our adieux, I completed a quick Google search for the rates, and I reviewed my guidebook for any insider tips. I quickly noticed the Alexandra Hotel was a highly recommended dwelling. It was a grand old hotel with special packages for West Highland Wayers.

I decided on history and chose the Alexandra Hotel. As I entered the entrance way upon marble floors, I inquired about the special package. The cost was about $10 extra than the Premier Inn, however, because of the timeworn décor, I agreed. I had to wait a few hours before I could check in because of my arrival time. Wonderfully, the Alexandra Hotel allowed me to stash my backpack while I meandered around Fort William to kill the time.

Fort William was a delightful surprise to the system. As expected, it extended foods, dwelling establishments, souvenir boutiques peddling local handicrafts, and walkways on which to waddle and dawdle; practically all of it strewn along a single, astoundingly cobblestoned street. The street was a pedestrian only route named High Street. It provided an eclectic taste, an atmosphere from a Charles Dickens novel. I was eager to have a look. As I strolled unhurriedly up and down High Street, I noted a mixture of locals and tourists. I noticed a few with their cameras bouncing around their necks, others consuming ice-cream, or predominantly, individuals parading into and out of the sovereign shops.

The stunning aspect of Fort William. I roamed around without my backpack, unburdened. I could walk fully erect. My eyes were staring around and up instead of predominantly down at the ground. I strode towards the Loch Linnhe. The earlier mountains and trails were now simply backdrops. After stopping for a harmonious moment, I soaked up the breathtaking scenery I had come so far to see. I thought to myself, "I journey for wonder, bliss, and peace." The West Highland Way obliged me to accomplish that pursuit. "I had gawked at my fears and made them shrink backward. I was stronger, which brought me further harmony."

Before traveling back to Glasgow in a few days, I contemplated pushing forward along the Great Glen Way. It was another seventy-five miles ahead. However, I only had five days to accomplish it and return to Glasgow for my flight home to Florida. Unfortunately, after researching the analytics of travel, I realized I could not pursue the trek. The train only left in return to Glasgow from the endpoint. I concluded I could not average roughly twenty miles a day to complete the journey.

As time neared for check-in, I retired to the hotel.

That night, I slumbered soundly. I was happy convincing myself I was a good and brave man. By accomplishing the West Highland Way, I was powerful. I was the master of my destiny. Partaking on trips like this, (3rd one, *A Quest for St. James* and *Rambling Across America*), I was facing life courageously.

*"We only live once, Snoopy," said Charlie Brown,
"wrong, we only die once. We live every day."*
—Snoopy

*"We must be willing to let go of the life we planned
so as to have the life that is waiting for us."*
—Joseph Campbell

CHAPTER 25

FORT WILLIAM TO GLASGOW

I awoke for the last day of my two-night rest in Fort William. I had the fragments of a dream tugging me back towards sleep. After repacking my backpack and checking out, I strolled a few blocks to the train station to board my transport back to Glasgow.

The seat I secured on the train was facing the outside world. I could sit at a table seat, meaning there were four seats and a table between them. I set up my camera on my tripod and faced it out the window, and placed my journal on the table to write any last inspirational thoughts.

As the landscapes passed by from my train seat, I smirked at the suddenness with which my circumstances had changed. Eleven days of walking equated to a rapid few hours' train ride because of the various stops it had to incur. However, I enjoyed the quick memories returned when I saw places I recently was walking upon. I had walked over 125-miles since my departure from Glasgow.

"The more I study nature, the more I stand amazed at the work of the Creator."
—Louis Pasteur

"Everything you ever wanted is one step outside your comfort zone."
—Unknown

CHAPTER 26

GLASGOW TO TPA

When I awakened to the early alarm, I collected my belongings and headed out onto the darkened streets. I strolled to George Square. On a previous day, I inquired of a location to catch the bus to the airport. Nervously, I noticed roadwork around the square, which was detouring all traffic. I was concerned it may mean it would deviate the public bus. I chatted with a police person, and they recommended I walk to the bus station. It was an extra mile I did not foresee to walk. The good news was I had plenty of time.

As I arrived at the bus terminal, I sat fidgety, expecting my ride to the airport. I continued to stare upon the arriving and departing buses, infused with anxiety I would miss it or climb on the incorrect one.

Returning to the Glasgow airport was bittersweet, since my trip was in its final stages. Yet I cherished the adventure. I was sad I was returning to the US. I continued to ask the Universe I could travel and write full time. I was in complete joy on my expeditions.

Readying for takeoff, the motors revved to peak capacity. The pilots throttled up as we rumbled forward. The thrust built quickly. We scampered forward swiftly. Abruptly, the thundering underneath the tires calmed. The vibrations detected through my upright posture were alleviated. The nose raised skyward. We climbed. I was departing Scotland.[5]

"I can't change the direction of the wind, but I can adjust my sails to always reach my destination."
—Jimmy Dean

CHAPTER 27

TAMPA, FL

The aircraft tires chirped as they tagged the tarmac. As I withdrew from the United airplane, I was once again in Tampa, Florida. The Tampa International Airport train drew to a stop. When the mechanical doors slid open, I strode towards the escalator. I descended, and I strolled to the baggage claim.

I disliked I was back. There was a surge of unknown for me. I aspired to linger on a trek somewhere. I returned to the reality of being jobless, with the same inner strife. Either make Tommy Ray Entertainment successful or return to a day job as a physician assistant. Sadly, though, the current state of Tommy Ray Entertainment only allowed a Big Mac once a month. To conduct what I wished, I had to push forward to landing a day job to collect and receive financial rewards in order to pursue my dream life. Writing, editing, recording, marketing creates a heavy price tab. The last option would become homeless.

I had adequate finances to last until early November. I knew daily I would endure to grind on the Tommy Ray Entertainment Brand.

After gathering my backpack encased in its duffel bag. I texted my oldest brother John to pick me up in his white van. Upon entering the four-wheel coffin, we headed to his home. A kind gesture to allow me to stick around until a new day job arose or I could create a miracle with Tommy Ray Entertainment.

"Trust yourself. You have survived a lot, and you will survive whatever is coming."
—Robert Tew

"Making a big life change is scary, but you know what's even scarier? Regret."
—Zig Ziglar

"Expose yourself to your deepest fear. After that, fear has no power, and fear of freedom shrinks and vanishes. You are free."
—Jim Morrison

CHAPTER 28

From time to time, I was asked why I went on those adventures, especially alone. First thought, I was single. Besides that, I would enjoy a companion and hope one day to have someone able and wanting to tag along with me. The other feelings were I loved being in open nature, observing wildlife and being in awe of majestic landscapes or marvelous architecture.

I do grow weary every so often on the trail, but still moved forward one step at a time. I enjoyed the endless slog each day. I kept the curiosity of a child to see what may be over the next peak.

In 2012, I slept in albergues every night. In 2016, my Toyota Tacoma was my home, mostly. On the West Highland Way, I slept predominantly in a tent. I savored all and would continue throughout all future trips, chiefly, based on where I may be on my adventure.

"Carry in your memory for the rest of your life the good things that came out of those difficulties. They will serve as a proof of your abilities and will give you confidence when you are faced by other obstacles."
—Unknown

CHAPTER 29

Overall, the West Highland Way did not disappoint. I was elated, as well as immensely appreciative of being out there. True blessings were the open landscapes which predominated the West Highland Way. I never perceived being trapped in impenetrable woods. I ended up hiking up mountains, along lonely paths, through various sheep grazing pastures which extended splendid views of distant summits, over sharp rocky trails, mile after endless mile of majestic Scottish Highlands.

The route varied from large enough for a truck to pass and was as narrow as eighteen inches wide. One warning I have for you, my readers: even on sunny days, the route could be a running stream. I experimented successfully wearing my Lone Peak 4.0's with waterproof socks. I was delighted to say I had no blisters and my feet remained dry no matter how many streams I crossed or mud I trudged through. I vowed not to succumb to soggy feet, smelly feet, or sodden socks.

Another blessing of the Scotland adventure was the ability to wild camp openly except for a limited section.

"If we can see past perceived limitations, then the possibilities are endless."
—Amy Purdy

CHAPTER 30

I had set out to achieve something fearless, and I had done precisely that. By concluding my adventure, I demonstrated to myself I was capable of immense accomplishments. I accepted I could launch myself into fantastic accomplishments in all phases of my life. There were no challenges too great for me to welcome. Beyond any doubt, those treks did not happen every day. I drank up every final drop.

By completing the West Highland Way, I trusted I reached a purified, more organic state of being. I gained great knowledge of how to have bliss in life's simple pleasures.[5]

As I conclude this travel memoir of the West Highland Way, I, as of now, discover myself imagining back to the time where I measured the day by the position of the sun, my stomach growls, or weariness.[7] The minicomputer I wear on my wrist is a reminder I belong as an adventurer by heart, instead of a chained lost soul to the matrix. The positive, as I think about my experiences with love and sentimentality, I realize the next experience is an uncomplicated decision. I have demonstrated to myself and others I can do anything I put in my mind to. Essentially, "go do it" was the formula.

A treasured lesson learned from the West Highland Way was the encounters, the recollections, the awesome triumphant delight of living to the fullest degree in which I found genuine meaning. God, I am genuinely thankful for being alive.[9]

"I have not tired of the wilderness; rather I enjoy its beauty. I prefer the star-sprinkled sky to a roof, the obscure and difficult trail leading to the unknown, to any paved highway. I feel I belong and am one with the world around me. I am surrounded by beauty. I know I could not bear the routine and humdrum of the life that many are forced to lead. I have known too much of the depths of life already."
—Everett Ruess

INSPIRATIONAL RESOURCES

1.) Jenkins, Jedidiah, *To Shake the Sleeping Self* (2018; Convergent Books)
2.) Loram & Thomas, *West Highland Way* (2016; Trailblazer Publications)
3.) Adams, Mark, *Tip of the Iceberg* (2019; Dutton)
4.) King, Stephen, *The Shining* (1977; Anchor Books)
5.) Davidson, Jim, *The Next Everest* (2021; St. Martin's Press)
6.) https://www.mountaineering.scot/safety-and-skills/health-and-hygiene/ticks
7.) Davis, Zach, *Appalachian Trials* (2012; Good Badger Publishing)
8.) Bryson, Bill, *A Walk in the Woods* (2010; Crown
9.) Jenkins, Peter, *A Walk Across America* (2001; Mariner Books)
10.) King, Stephen, *Doctor Sleep* (2013; Gallery Books)

ABOUT THE AUTHOR

Born in rural Mississippi, Tommy Ray grew up with a desire to write books, sing songs and explore the world. And so, he has.

Tommy Ray chose to become an author to create value and inspiration for the world. He desires all to leave their mark, emphasizing that you should not take this life for granted. Having always been inspired by travel adventure tales of real-life journeys, Tommy firmly believes that you should never give up on your dreams.

Tommy's always had a voice inside of him telling him to live his life through creativity. For many years he ignored the voice to follow other endeavors, but the voice was always there and increasing in volume. As Tommy loves to travel, write, compose songs and perform them he decided that the artist's way was the one in which he desired to spend his life.

To add to his oeuvre, he recently created the Amid the Blackness series. These are a series of short stories which fall in the suspense/horror fiction category. So far Tommy has published the first 3 stories in Amid the Blackness – Mirror Of Perception, The Insane Ins*ide*, *Feast Of The Werewolf.* All are available on Amazon Kindle.

Keep a lookout for upcoming music from Tommy Ray – both country and alternative rock. Tommy writes and sings his own original songs and has been intent on doing so ever since when he was an infant at a Georgia kindergarten: here he stood up and announced to his classmates and teacher that he wanted to grow up to "drive trucks, drink beer and sing country songs." His priorities may have changed somewhat but his desire to sing remains true.

This Country Boy from small-town Mississippi is making giant strides across the world: Tommy Ray is a rising talent in American literature and music – check him out!

www.tommyrayentertainment.com

SOCIAL MEDIA

Facebook:
https://www.facebook.com/TRayEnterntainment

Twitter:
https://twitter.com/TRayEntertainm2

Instagram:
https://www.instagram.com/t_ray_entertainment/

I invite you to continue keeping up with me at:
www.tommyrayentertainment.com

Do Not Miss Future Adventures with Tommy Ray

I ask and invite you to leave a review on the purchasing website.

"Country Boy Travel Series"

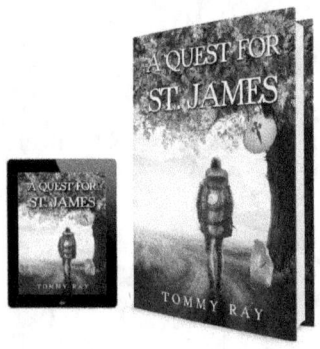

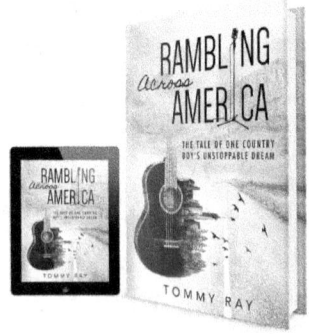

"Amid the Blackness" Series

Short stories to allow a glimpse into
the nightmares of Tommy Ray

"You cannot go back and change the beginning, but you can start from where you are and change the end."
—C.S. Lewis

"I believe my music is my inner voice screaming aloud, expressing my emotion, thoughts, and life experiences. I like to write about what I feel. Throughout stylistic shifts, my signature wrasp, unwavering melody, and down-to-business songwriting tether together for the brilliant steps into the hearts of music fans the world over. Numerous music critics have written my music is "a ride worth taking."

www.ingramcontent.com/pod-product-compliance
Lightning Source LLC
Chambersburg PA
CBHW071237070526
44583CB00017B/2226